THE GUIDEBOOK COLLECTION OF TRANSFORMING: UNLEARNING / UNDOING / CREATING

SERIES 1: THE GROUNDWORK (PREPARATION)

VIRGINIA ANNE

BALBOA.
PRESS

A DIVISION OF HAY HOUSE

Balboa Press books may be ordered through booksellers or by contacting:

Balboa Press
A Division of Hay House
1663 Liberty Drive
Bloomington, IN 47403
www.balboapress.com
1 (877) 407-4847

Because of the dynamic nature of the Internet, any web addresses or links contained in this book may have changed since publication and may no longer be valid. The views expressed in this work are solely those of the author and do not necessarily reflect the views of the publisher, and the publisher hereby disclaims any responsibility for them.

The author of this book does not dispense medical advice or prescribe the use of any technique as a form of treatment for physical, emotional, or medical problems without the advice of a physician, either directly or indirectly. The intent of the author is only to offer information of a general nature to help you in your quest for emotional and spiritual well-being. In the event you use any of the information in this book for yourself, which is your constitutional right, the author and the publisher assume no responsibility for your actions.

Any people depicted in stock imagery provided by Thinkstock are models, and such images are being used for illustrative purposes only.
Certain stock imagery © Thinkstock.

Print information available on the last page.

ISBN: 978-1-5043-4221-6 (sc)
ISBN: 978-1-5043-4222-3 (e)

Balboa Press rev. date: 11/16/2015

Lovingly Dedicated To:

Those who endured and endure
mistreatment, trauma and abuse.
May these pages help set you free!

***

Alexandra

Your drive and determination is an inspiration.
I am forever blessed with the gift of a beautiful daughter.

***

Dr. Mary Kannankeril

What can I say?
My co-creator, my teacher.
The person who tore me loose from my nightmare.
I am forever grateful.

***

Lisa

May you acquire the courage to live fully as Lisa.

***

CONTENTS

PREFACE

The Guidebook Collection of Transforming: Unlearning/Undoing/ Creating came into being after I was "forced" to finally face long buried abuse/trauma from early childhood. Past memories surfaced and I started on a healing path which I am still walking and will be until my God calls me home. The changes I have made, how differently I think and feel today is opposite to the way I was raised.

I discovered that we can overcome what happened to us. We can fix ourselves. There are some of us so attached to our pain and misery, we refuse to give it up. We are so identified with who we are, the thought of changing ourselves is too terrifying for some.

I wrote these guidebooks to help those who are making inner changes and are expelling past or present trauma/abuse. I have walked the walk. I experienced firsthand what it is like to feel long-held repressed emotions for the first time. I know what it is like to live with PTSD (Post Traumatic Stress Disorder) that I had for over one year. I know how it feels to remember horrific memories. I know what it is like to have so many parts within all scattered and running amok. And how I integrated all my parts into one. The panic I have experienced is indescribable. The hurt, anger, rage, frustration. The rejection. The control tactics used on me. The brainwashing.

I also know how to be free of this long held prison sentence. I know how to process memories and be unattached to them. I took the steps needed to overcome the PTSD. I know what it feels like to be free. I know the unraveling of layer upon layer. We do not need to be a victim, we survived and we can thrive. Does this mean I am now perfect and free from everything? Of course not, this is a work in progress. The benefit, though, to walking this walk is how we become freer, wiser, and calmer, which leads to our ultimate goal. To be better attuned to our true selves, to live the being side of a human being.

These guidebooks can be used by all ages. They can be used by those who were mistreated, who were traumatized, and who suffered all forms of abuse. I am not promising you a cure-all or a magic wand. What I am sharing with you are ways to overcome trauma; and to see life through a new set of eyes.

INTRODUCTION

Welcome to *The Guidebook Collection of Transforming: Unlearning/ Undoing/Creating*. This is the first of a series and is entitled, *The Groundwork (Preparation)*. This first guidebook is a synopsis of information to help you get started. Many of the subjects I cover in this guidebook can be books by themselves. This first guidebook is to give you a "flavor" of information and some obstacles and barriers you may encounter on your journey. It also includes self-starter helpers and helpful tools. As the name implies, this guide is to prepare you for the road ahead by providing groundwork.

The topics will be discussed in greater detail in the subsequent guidebooks. The list of topics I discuss in this first guidebook was discovered when walking my path of healing. I thought it would be great to provide a reference for those walking their own paths.

Taking full responsibility for your life is a necessary first step towards your healing. Ouch! That may sting some at first, but it is the crucial first step. Blaming others is so much easier, but gets you nowhere. Another crucial first step is accepting what happened to you, whether it was being ridiculed on a daily basis, or it was extreme forms of abuse. We cannot change what happened to us, but we sure can fix it. Regardless of who did what to you, it is fixable; you can create the life you deserve. And until you claim your life as yours, and take control of it, no permanent changes can be made. And that's what we want, permanent change, not a temporary fix.

So the question is, "Do you want to do what is necessary to get rid of, for good, the anguish and emptiness that is present within?" Have you ever wondered why you think and behave the way you do? Have you ever noticed your reactions or behaviors? We usually do not take notice of what we say, think or do. We do all these automatically like breathing. But we sure as heck notice what everyone else says and does, and we have plenty of opinions about it too!

Our current thoughts, behaviors, beliefs, and reactions are not etched in stone. Our brains are "moldable". We can "rewire" our brains, we can create healthy new brain pathways. Who we are has become normal for us. The way we think, talk, act is done unconsciously. For some of us, we believe the way we are, is the way it is.

We take our lot in life as permanent. "I can't change. I was born this way. This is how it is, oh well." We have molded ourselves into unchangeable human beings. Our cells constantly die and new ones are constantly born. Our skin sheds, our blood is constantly moving, and our organs work 24/7/365. Our bodies are in constant motion of cleansing, ridding, and renewing. Life is all about motion: creation, endings, beginnings, rebirth, renewal, growth, and change. Why then, can we not create something new for ourselves, in the way we speak, act, think, and believe? Be willing to allow new opportunities for yourself. Fear is what holds us back, it is fear that keep us from becoming who we deserve to be.

For many of us, we were taught that our external image matters more than our own internal workings. That how we are perceived matters more than how you feel about yourself; you come second, your image comes first. So we concentrate on the external world and making that look as good as we can while the inner longings and misery are continually pushed down and ignored. Ignoring your pain doesn't mean it goes away. It gets repressed, it gets pushed down, deep within. When something is ignored over time, it festers and demands attention. This repressed pain will try to get your attention by erupting in your external world through illness, relationship woes, less than desirable financial outcomes, a whole host of various addictions and obsessions, and/or whatever else that keeps you from living a life of wholeness and contentment.

You are not forever locked in your current thinking or behavioral patterns. You have choices. You can make changes. You may be living with unhealthy belief systems that you are not even aware of. You may be holding in your body, negative repressed emotions toward people and situations, and again you aren't even aware of it. Or you are aware, but do not know what to do about it.

This guidebook series serves to show you another way to be. You can be a different person, a healthier person, mentally and physically, though it all depends on you. You must have the desire to change. For your outer world will not change if no internal changes are made. You cannot change if you hold the same beliefs, opinions, and thoughts, as you always have. As the inner changes, the outer changes automatically.

If you are reading this, you most likely are in some form of pain be it emotional or physical. The process of healing and recovery can be taxing at times, and painful, but it is a productive pain. It moves through you whereas your daily pain is stagnant pain. The productive pain you experience is freeing you from the stagnant pain you now live with every day. Instead of just suffering and living with pain, you will be moving forward and away from it for good. The productive pain you experience is temporary while the stagnant pain is not.

The process of getting to know yourself is actually an unlearning process, an undoing, a peeling away of layer after layer. You cannot add anything to an already full body; you need to empty it first. I have tried many ways of changing and to no avail. Saying affirmations, by themselves, worked for me on a limited scale. I did not first remove the conflicting belief that I held about the affirmation. What I was affirming I did not believe. By getting down to the details of my thought processes was I able to rid myself of old, unhealthy beliefs. I was then able to instill new, healthy thoughts and beliefs. The old had to go before the new could enter.

You need to get rid of what is unhealthy inside you in order to heal and become the person you deserve to be. If you try to change without first dumping out the old, the new cannot enter – there is no room. You are too full of old patterns and beliefs. You may find empty "pockets" within you to fill with new thoughts, and changes may occur, but it usually is temporary or the changes are few and/or slight. What you want are significant permanent changes. As you move along you may be amazed that what you think and believe and see as "normal" is not "normal" at all. This is all you know, for you, it is "normal" and you will see how attached you are to your "normal" beliefs, attitudes, feelings, reactions, etc.

The best part about unlearning for me is, you do not have to try to control or change anyone else's feelings, opinions or reactions. You go inside yourself and learn about you, and change you - no one else, just you. You do not try to figure out why someone said this or that, or why this person reacted that way. Those things do not concern you anymore. What you do instead, is ask yourself why you reacted a certain way, why you said what you said, and be humble enough to accept the answer which comes from within.

No one has to know what you are doing. For example, if you are working on overcoming insecurities, no one has to know, only if you want them to. All the work is within and when you feel better, it shows externally. You allowed yourself to recognize within, the true extent of your insecurities.

We all possess the same traits and behaviors. The difference is some traits are stronger or more extreme in certain individuals. We are judgmental, know-it-alls, braggers, egotists, conceited, selfish, and opinionated. We all have them, some less than others and some more than others. We all have weaknesses we need to recognize in ourselves. How do we recognize these things? By taking off the blinders. You may not like what you see, but when you see it clearly and can accept it, than a transformation can take place.

Ask yourself, "Why do I act this way? Why did I respond like that? Was my reaction over the top?" This newfound information about yourself may hurt, and it may sting at first. By acknowledging your weaknesses, they begin to weaken. Learn the steps to recognize and become aware of yourself. Admitting you are selfish, for example, and doing nothing about it does not change a thing. There are those who enjoy their selfishness and refuse to give it up since they are so identified with that aspect of themselves. It is how they know themselves to be – it is their "normal" and they won't budge.

Know with certainty all answers lie within, happiness lies within, as does peace and contentment. Happiness is not something we obtain from the outer world. It is something we are within, it is a state of being. We need to stop focusing on outside influences, situations, and relationships. It is about making you a better person, for when the inside is polished clean the outside shines as bright. I am not saying your troubles will magically vanish. What will change is your thought process and your reaction. Instead of having the problem consume you and overwhelm you, you can step back and look at it from a higher perspective.

> When we can be humble and declare "We know nothing" and are willing to listen and learn from our inner selves, then the gate opens wide.

> When we can be humble and declare "Yes I am judgmental" or selfish or whatever then we gain the courage to remove the blinders.

> When we can be humble enough to cease to control, and allow a Higher Source to show us the way, then we change so much that we are not the same person.

So, let's begin your journey of recovery and healing! This process goes at your speed and no one else's. Baby steps at times will be mandatory, while other times you may experience giant leaps and bounds. These guidebooks were written as a tool and a reference to aid you on your journey. It takes time and patience to learn and master certain steps.

This series in no way replaces or substitutes any medical assistance. I am not a medical professional. If you need help, seek it out. Do not be afraid to find a professional you can work with. Each one has their specialty and you want to be with the right person when it comes to your medical health whether mental or physical. This guidebook series can be used as an adjunct to your current medical treatment and any current religious practices you are involved in. This series in no way takes you away from your religion. If you do not believe in a Higher Power or a One Universal Energy Source, do not let that stop you from healing; you deserve to heal no matter what.

"Where do I even begin?" you may ask yourself. It is a great question and one that may stop people from moving forward since they do not have any idea as to where to start. My goal is to help you get started; to equip you with tools, techniques, and insights I learned on my healing path, so you do not have to figure it out on your own.

This series sets the groundwork to begin your inner changes. These collections of guidebooks are written to help those that are sick and tired of their lives not working. They provide an easy to follow format on clearing out the old once and for all and to instill the new. In other words, getting rid of unhealthy: thinking, false beliefs, attitudes, feelings and emotions and replacing them with healthy ones.

You are at the very beginning of who you are truly meant to be. Let your journey begin!

SECTION 1

GROUNDING INFORMATION (BEFORE WE DIG)

CHILD EMOTIONS/ HANDLING EMOTIONS

Before my healing began, I did not know how to express anger. I held it in. Then an event would trigger something inside me and out it came, not anger but rage. My reaction was over and above a "normal" angry response. I had years of stored anger within, but was unaware that I did.

As a child I was not allowed to express anger. I was raised with the "children are seen and not heard" mentality. When I felt anger as a child I had to keep it in and was not allowed to express it either physically or verbally. Holding in my anger became a practice for me. Years go by and now we are adults, but the anger from childhood still resides within. Plus holding in the anger is still practiced as an adult; it's all you know. You may have forgotten about your childhood anger, but it hasn't left your body, it's still there. As an adult, I had a stockpile of unexpressed anger in my body.

Memories and feelings are stored in both mind and body. My consciousness did not know it existed, but my subconscious knew. I had myself convinced that I did not have anger issues, but after conferring with a professional, I felt it was time for me to explore this area. When I left the doctor's office, I told my body it was okay for any repressed anger to come to the surface now. I said it was safe to do so and nothing bad would happen. I put it out of my mind and on the third day I had this internal shaking in my arms. It scared me at first because I didn't know what it was. I then realized it was the anger coming up to my conscious state. It was the anger starting to loosen and be released. I was amazed.

It came like a tsunami hitting land. All this rage came bursting out of me; it wasn't anger, it was pure, raw rage; and lots of it. I was enraged like never before. I screamed, I punched the air and I banged a pillow with a book over and over. I was in control of my senses during all this and was not about to punch anyone or the wall. It wasn't about including the innocent. It was about me releasing years of pent up rage. I allowed the body to lead the way and it released as much rage as it could handle. Things settled down and the next day it started up again. This time I knew what to expect and I allowed it to be what it was.

As I released the rage that festered in me, my outer rage subsided. So if I got angry, I got angry and not enraged like I did in the past. I released so much and I did so in a healthy and safe way. I felt the rage, I expressed it, I acknowledged it, and I didn't repress it anymore. After things settled down, I actually felt hollowness inside my legs. I knew it meant that I had gotten rid of so much, it actually emptied out of my body, and I could feel it!

After past anger is released, the goal is to keep future anger out. Any new anger-promoting events need to be dealt with, in the present time, and not stored away and repressed yet again. I did not know how to be angry but my doctor explained that first and foremost you need to vent the anger but not on the person who angered you. You need to acknowledge the anger and not deny it. If you must get it out by talking, then tell a trusted friend, but do not tell the whole neighborhood. Write it out, or go exercise. If you can remain calm when the person angers you then you can try the following:

> Compliment the person to show it is not them
> you are addressing, it is their behavior. Then

describe the event that angered you. Finish with something like, "I appreciate it if you don't do that again or I prefer you not behave that way again."

I refer to it as learning emotional maturity. For many of us, we get defensive when someone hurts us and we attack back. There are also many of us who recoil and shut down. You may need a day or two for the anger to settle before you can even approach the person. There are those who cannot express themselves, let alone approach someone. If possible, try to wait for your feelings to calm. Handling angry emotions is definitely a work in progress! When you give yourself the gift of self-awareness, the need for anger in your life decreases. The higher your thinking, the less need there is for anger.

I now know it is not others who are causing the anger, it is my reaction that is causing it. "They" are triggering something in me I need to fix. We all get angry and overreact from time to time. If you emotionally overreact on a frequent basis, then perhaps it's time to ask yourself why and/or to seek professional guidance. An overreaction can be caused by a trigger. Something is being activated within that is stirring up past experiences. You may not even remember those experiences, but I have found people can and do find the trigger source.

Let's say your father was an alcoholic and would come home drunk, his breath stinking of a certain beer brand, and he would beat you. As an adult, one night you are out with friends. One friend gets drunk and in your face and it's the same smell as your father's breathe. If the smell is on the subconscious level and not the conscious level, something within will trigger from the smell. Maybe you pick a fight with your friend or you need to go home because suddenly you do not feel well. Perhaps you no longer wish to be friends, you don't know why – you just don't want to speak with him anymore. Or maybe something ever so slight gets stirred inside, like something feels different or weird but you cannot put your finger on it; something just isn't right.

A lot of us react and act from a child's point of view when confronted with stressful situations. Not every situation will cause us to become a kid again, but we do, at times, react emotionally as a child and I believe it's because we were not taught mature emotional thinking. No one teaches us how to transition from our underdeveloped emotions as children to a mature adult emotional level. Yes we become adults and mature but sometimes situations will cause us to revert back to childhood.

Let's say, you were ignored as a child. Maybe you had to say, "Mom" twenty or thirty times before she would answer you and when she did, she was angry with you for bothering her. You were not heard as a child. Now, chances are good, as an adult, you will couple up with someone who ignores you and gets annoyed when you bother them. This will trigger your past experience with Mom and could cause you to overreact and to do so in a childish way. It makes sense it would happen that way since you do not know any differently. You may not know how to react or respond. You may be unaware of the pattern you have developed in attracting people who ignore you since this is your "normal". This scenario could continue to repeat itself over and over in your life until you decide to face it. When you learn to identify your pattern(s), it becomes easier for you to no longer need people in your life that ignore you. If these people do enter your life, you no longer have a desire or a need to be in their company.

For some men, feelings and emotions are one tough nut for them to crack. They are taught that "boys don't cry", and that "boys are tough and rugged" and that feelings are for "sissies and girls". And if a boy cries, you would think he committed a felony. It is sad how we deny our children to fully express their feelings and emotions. And for some women out there, emotions and feelings were not an option growing up. "Stop acting like a baby" was a big one for a lot of us, male and female. And there are those that are so disconnected from their feelings and emotions that they just don't feel.

Are we locked into this mess forever? No. Part of the journey is feelings; you need to feel in order to heal. If this becomes too much, seek professional help, you need not do this on your own. Get help if you are crying out for it; seek out a trusted counselor, a medical professional, or a support group. I could not have healed without my doctor's guidance, advice, input, insight and assistance.

On our path of healing, emotions and memories may become overwhelming at times, especially in the beginning, when we are allowing ourselves to feel feelings we have not felt before. Your natural reaction is to become a kid again and have the emotions and feelings overwhelm you and overpower you. This is where you need to tell yourself that you are an adult. You are no longer the child. You need not let these feelings get the better of you. You need to feel the child's feelings and you can do so from an adult standpoint and this includes feeling the anger, the grief, the sadness and letting the tears flow.

If you feel overwhelmed just tell yourself, "Perhaps I am overwhelmed right now and need to break, to take my mind off of this for right now. I will return when my strength returns." Be gentle with yourself, know you will have down times; you need them in order to move forward. Don't give up because things get a little rough. Hang in there, back off, but come back. You are heading home to where you belong, and all of this will be behind you for good. Get over one hurdle and then you get over another and another.

THE DIVINE

This is where my heart lies – to live as the being I truly am. As you progress, your focus shifts from external to internal. You live your life from within which shines outward. This has nothing to do with religion. It has all to do with awakening, of living the life of being. My path includes the Divine at my side every step of the way. There were times when I was carried by unseen forces.

The name God has become an overused term for some, not the meaning, but the word itself; that the word God has lost its sacredness. Look at how it is used today; omg is so common; we use "Oh My God" as an exclamation. There is nothing sacred in omg. The name God isn't even capitalized anymore, we have diminished the name to a small g.

For some people the mere mention of God sends them into terror. For some of us, we heard how God was going to punish us and send us to hell. Some of us laughed it off, others were terrorized by it. God was pictured as this revengeful King sitting on a throne throwing down lightning bolts to those who dared go outside the dictates of the religion. When you understand that it was a control tactic, than perhaps your perception of God can be redirected into a loving understanding of this indescribable Higher Power.

People have been sexually abused by church members and staff. Religion was used to instill fear, shame and guilt in order to control. There are people who don't believe in God, and there are people who cannot use the word because it triggers unpleasant memories for them. What we need to realize is that all of this is human inflicted and not God inflicted.

We cannot describe this Holy Power. This Power is so great, so vast, it is infinite. How can we possibly describe something of such magnitude, we cannot. This Higher Power can only be felt. This awesome energy that I call God wants only the best for us, for this energy unconditionally loves us, cares for and about us, and wants a relationship with us. He is the reason I exist for He created me. Why would God create something he would not love? That is not how God operates.

Don't get hung up on what one calls this Higher Power. It is Indescribable, so use any word, name, or phrase that makes you feel comfortable. Use words or phrases that resonate deep within you; that gives you peace and calmness within. If you don't believe in a Higher Source or you cannot deal with it, by no means let that stop you from healing. I personally do not have a problem with using the name God, but the list of describing this awesome power is varied for those who cannot connect to the word God: Energy, Energy Source, The Light, Being, Higher Power, The Infinite, The Universe, The Divine, Divine Source, Love, All That Is, The Indescribable, are only a few. What is most important is what this Power represents. When I suggest to use another name, Energy for example, for this Higher Power, I am referring to an Energy of love, of wisdom, an infinite, indescribable presence. I am not reducing God down to Energy such as electrical, etc.

As humans we live in a world of polarities: up/down, in/out, yin/yang, bitter/sweet, etc. God is above polarities, He is both male and female. I try not to use a pronoun but if I do, I use Him when I refer to God, it is just my preference. Don't get hung up on the name, get hung up on all that this awesome, indescribable power provides us.

The magical garden of The Divine is where I experience my deepest feelings of love, peace, happiness, joy, and contentment. Nothing at all in the external world can even come close to the loving profoundness of this Unseen World. This is not a place you visit; it is who you are underneath it all. It is you as "being." There is nothing but the Creator, and this Force loves us unconditionally and only wants the best for us.

EMPTINESS

I think a lot of people can relate to a feeling of a void within, something is missing but we don't know what. It is like a bottomless pit that cannot be filled. This emptiness inside is not connected to a certain event or anything solid. It is just there. The subtle depression and the being down. Not having our way, but not even knowing what way we want.

This underlying pull of: pain, emptiness, loneliness, sorrow, guilt, regret, anxiety, desire, nameless hunger, yearning, craving, longing, wanting, and waiting does not cease. We either run from it or try to numb it. You do not know the source; it's just there, it feels like eternal emptiness. When life is going well it is quiet. It gets activated when we are bored, depressed, lonely, frustrated, angry, sad, and when situations do not go our way. This is different from breaking up with someone or losing a job; those emotions are acute and temporary whereas the emptiness is chronic.

I learned from this emptiness that I was not utilizing the other half of me – the **being** side of human. We are a human being and I was living a life of a human and very little of a being. I was looking for the problems to go away on the outside. I did not know my life would change by changing my thoughts and that the answers were within and not without.

The bottom line, it is love, not romantic love, but a higher, pure form of love. It is unconditional. Over the ages we lost and diminished our being side. The most fantastic part about walking this path is how much you grow and learn; it's amazing. You may go through turmoil by processing outdated emotions, but once you do, you are awakened into a higher phase of living, knowing and learning. You become aware that you are part of an infinite loving universe.

Forgiveness

I thought forgiveness was condoning the behavior; that the offender was not getting their due justice. That he/she was getting away with hurting me and I wasn't about to let that happen. This person was to be in agony in my heart and mind forever; suffered and tortured all the rest of their days. The problem was, all this was happening inside my head and the only one that was being tortured was myself. Forgiveness to me meant letting them get away with it, receiving a verdict of not guilty. I held rage, bitterness, and hatred toward the people who hurt me. Forgiveness was not an option.

I thought forgiving the person meant liking the person. You cannot force yourself to like anyone, and is not necessary for forgiving. This alone helped me enormously knowing I did not have to speak to the person again nor was I forced to like them. It is not about like or dislike, it is about releasing the pain inflicted upon you. You no longer need to be attached to the person(s) who hurt you by staying in unforgiving mode. It does not mean you will forget the event. It means you are no longer attached to these people or to the event. Some people experience guilt and/or shame if they do not forgive someone. They have a belief that they must forgive in order to be a "good" person.

In some religious and self-help circles, forgiveness is the first thing we <u>must</u> do. Talk about pressure. It can be a daunting task for some, especially if we are not equipped with knowledge about forgiveness. It adds pressure to do the "right" thing. Doing the "right" thing does not help in our healing. In order to heal, we must feel long-held emotions buried within. These need to rise to the surface for processing. When we forgive someone before this is accomplished, it sets up a wall that blocks our progress. Now that we forgave the person, we do not have to feel the feelings. And how can we truly forgive if we are holding powerful resentment within towards this person?

Forgiveness comes; but it comes at the end of processing our feelings, our thoughts, and our reactions to the incident that hurt us. If we forgive someone first, we stop our healing. We do not process what needs to be felt in order to heal. Process your feelings, acquire knowledge, gain the wisdom necessary, and forgiveness comes naturally and on its own. For once you wrap your mind, body and heart around the injustice; this allows compassion, understanding, and forgiveness to shine through.

Do not beat yourself up because you cannot forgive someone this very moment. Do the work, it will come. Do not forgive the person at a surface level and shut out your healing; go through the process and you will be amazed at the insights you will uncover. You will experience how forgiveness does set you free, and how amazing deep-felt forgiveness feels. When I felt forgiveness for the first time, it was so deep and so real. I could feel compassion, understanding, and forgiveness. I was set free.

While I was doing my healing work, I included affirmations that included forgiveness. I didn't feel forgiveness, but I needed to start allowing the forgiveness to slowly soak through to my subconscious. And for others, forgiveness is deeply felt almost immediately, follow your body, it knows. Just be sure you are not using forgiveness to circumvent your healing or to bury your feelings.

There were some painful episodes in my life, as an adult, where I was betrayed and treated unfairly. I held hatred and rage against these people for a long time. I could not let them go, the hate was intense. During my healing, I discovered that the primary energy that I emitted was one of rejection. I was unaware of this my entire life. I discovered that my primary caretaker used rejection in order to control me which began in early childhood. This was all I knew, to be rejected was normal for me.

It became easier to forgive these people since I saw my input into the situation. What they did to me was most unfair, but I accepted my (unconscious) role in it, and was finally able to let the situation go. I am no longer bound to these people, the cords have been cut. Though I forgave them, that doesn't mean I like them or agree with how they handled the situation. By forgiving them and letting them go, they are now non-existent in my inner life and are unable to cause me any more emotional or physical pain. It is a wonderful feeling to be free from those who injured you mentally, physically, or financially.

Many theories, opinions, and how-to books are written about forgiveness. I tried various ways and methods; the one that worked for me was doing the inner work, to learn what made me tick. I needed to unlearn, undo, and instill new and healthy belief systems. I realized these people were not worth being inside me and causing me ills, both mentally and physically.

Forgiveness Reminders:

- To be willing to forgive is half the battle.
- Forgiving the person first can be an obstacle to your healing.
- You are forgiving the person and not condoning the behavior.
- You need not like the person you are forgiving.
- You need not forgive the person to their face. You are forgiving them for your sake.
- By not working on your healing, you stay attached to the person who hurt you through your resentment, bitterness and anger against what they did to you. Do you really want to stay "hooked" into this person?
- Be willing to forgive yourself. Be grateful for whom you are right now.
- Refusing to forgive yourself can be due to spiritual pride or lack of self-regard.
- Past mistakes and errors are lessons to be learned and not behaviors to repeat.
- Understand that hurting another stems from selfishness.

HUMILITY

"The greatest barrier is man's assumption
he already knows the answers to his problems."
Vernon Howard

Don't ever assume you already have the answers.

The practice of being humble, of being modest is a priority. Being humble is not being proud or arrogant. Allow yourself to be emptied of any preconceived ideas, notions, or answers in order for new insights to enter. "I do not know the answers" should be your foundation for learning. If you think you already know the answers then what you are doing is blocking the answers you need.

For example, "Well my parents beat me, that's why I am the way I am." Yes, your parents beat you, "but you are the way you are" due to your reaction (your thoughts and feelings) at the time of the incident. Chances are you could not express those thoughts and feelings at the time and so you repressed them. Those thoughts and feelings have not left you. Until they are acknowledged and released, they will remain in the body and can manifest as either mental or physical ailments.

Yes you were beaten, but what keeps you stuck and trapped in your life of misery is to keep ignoring what is inside you. What sets you free is to feel the feelings and emotions that existed when the incident(s) occurred.

The body needs to release these toxic feelings. Some resistance statements you may tell yourself:

"I know I should but I can't."
"It hurts too much."
"It's too emotional."
"I don't know how to handle my emotions."
"I don't know how to feel my feelings."
"I'm terrified to feel what I may feel."

Yes there is fear, how could there not be? It is one's desire that overcomes the fear factor. My willingness to allow my body to lead me in healing, led me to clearer vision, deeper insights, and a changed way of thinking and believing. Do you have to process every incident that happened to you? No.

Every day, make it a fresh start, be a beginner, a novice, because in essence, that is where you are. You will move forward, sometimes by leaps and bounds, and most times slow and steady. What happens is as you grow and learn, you ascend to another level of insight. By being on this new level you are, again, a beginner. By adopting the "I don't know" mentality and telling yourself "I am a beginner in all of this" you will get the answers you need because you are leaving yourself open for insight to enter.

When we tell ourselves "I don't know" we are then willing to listen and learn from our inner selves. A gentle attitude of "let me get out of my own way" in order to receive this invaluable information will do wonders for your journey forward. Be humble, be modest, do not be haughty or arrogant, and do not possess the "I know it all" attitude. So allow yourself to relax, to realize that all is well and that great insights are now heading your way.

KNOWLEDGE
KNOWLEDGE IS NOT WISDOM

Knowledge in and of itself does not cause inner change, but serves as a catalyst to change. You know in your head that man or woman is no good for you, and you may have a mental desire to leave the unhealthy situation, but you stay with them anyway because deep down, the desire is not in your heart. When the desire and knowledge soaks into the heart and body, then steps will be taken to find the way to leave.

Permanent change happens when knowledge and desire is known and felt in both mind and body (heart). You have a desire in your head to quit smoking but the desire is not in your heart. So you may try again and again without success, or you may quit only to replace it with another addiction. When the desire is both in your head and in your heart then permanent solutions are possible.

Have you ever had a light bulb moment that went off inside your head and you instantly got it and felt it at the same time? You changed instantly due to that awakening, that realization. I wish all changes could be instantaneous, but for some changes to take effect, it takes time and patience for the realization to sink down into the body and become a part of you.

Deep, ingrained beliefs we have about ourselves, and the identities we cling to, are deeply rooted within. We have a desire in our mind to unlearn and undo these beliefs and so we begin. The desire may not be in our hearts just yet, but will catch up and soak in as time goes by. Even for extreme abuse cases, if the desire to fix yourself is strong enough, then it is doable. Some unlearning and undoing may require extra attention and time, but that doesn't mean it cannot be done.

Having knowledge in the brain is one half of the equation. Realizing that your abandonment issues come from your mother leaving you at an early age is the first stage. This stage is a huge step for people for it finally links their behavior to a source. This can be so freeing in and of itself. The next stage is having that knowledge soak into your whole being so you finally rid yourself of being involved in relationships, where eventually, your partner walks out on you. We need to keep reenacting our childhood experiences, since this is all we know, until we eradicate the need to repeat it over and over.

How is this done? It is a process that requires unraveling down to the core of what makes you tick. This is what this guidebook collection entails: the process of unlearning, undoing, letting go, rebuilding, rewiring, renewing, creating, and transforming yourself into the person you deserve to be. To feel the gratification of your own successful inner changes and achievements is indescribable.

I want to point out that blame is not mentioned. Did you read anywhere where I blamed the parents or caregivers or myself, that, "If it wasn't for them, _____." There is no time for blame; blame is resistance. What matters is, we want to fix what is broke inside regardless of how it got there. When we accept ourselves whole-heartedly, we discover love within ourselves we did not know we had. We discover a love for self and love for others. As we transform our less than desirable traits, thoughts and beliefs, we start to view life from a higher perspective.

THE LAW OF ATTRACTION

The Law of Attraction has gained in popularity. Many people believe in it, many do not believe in it, and there are people who don't understand how it works.

The Law of Attraction is constantly working in our lives. We attract to us what we need to keep feeding our identity, our belief system, and how we truly feel about ourselves. This is where people stop and do not want to take responsibility for their lives. This is where they want to blame the "other guy" for all the wrongs that come their way.

"My husband is a drunk so that's my fault?" No, it is not your fault that your husband is a drunk. What you are responsible for, is owning that you attracted him into your life. "He didn't start drinking until after we were married, when he lost his job...so I attracted that into my life?" As harsh as this may sound, yes you did. I am not blaming the wife or the husband, it is not about blame. It is about recognizing what you attract into your life.

People tend to look at the external factors and not the internal workings. What you attract on the outside reflects what is going on within. For a lot of people this is hard to swallow. Until you take full responsibility for your life and:

> stop the blame game
> get rid of the unhealthy stuff buried within you

start knowing that there are better ways to think
and believe
fix yourself
focus inward, not outward
you will continue to attract what you inner self
believes. You will not attract wealth to yourself if
your true feelings about money are negative and
that you feel deep within that you are not worthy
of being wealthy.

I overheard a conversation where this man was talking about
his sister-in-law and that she was married several times and how
each husband beat her. My first reaction was how amazing that
she attracted so many of them and they all fit her requirements.
If you keep attracting jobs you hate, people who are not good for
you, debt, illness, addictions, etc. than perhaps you could start
asking yourself why. "What's going on inside me to attract what
I attract?"

When you examine your past and present relationships, you
may see a pattern emerge, especially with intimate relationships,
as well as friendships, partnerships, and business associates. And
if you look even closer, you may see one of your parents or both
of them in your intimate relationships.

Remember, it is all you know, it is your "normal". List the
good and not so good qualities in your former partners. See the
similarities between them; this is what you are attracting on a
subconscious level. This is your pattern, your "normal". Do they
resemble one of your parents or are they the exact opposite? And
the uncanny part of this is that each one will get worse than the
prior one if no internal changes are made concerning your self-
worth. Bad boyfriend, the next one is worse. Bad job, the next
one is worse.

The Law of Attraction is an indicator of what you believe about yourself. What you think, how you feel, what you believe in comes to you whether good or bad. You are vibrating these things to you; change your vibration – change your world. The choices to learn more about The Law of Attraction are many. Find qualified authors and teachers on the subject if you wish to learn more; when the student is ready the teacher appears!

Normal

Our lives are our "normal" which are years of conditioning and programming instilled within to become who you are today. How you act, react, think, feel, behave, believe, is your "normal". It is all you know. And for a good part of us, anyone outside our own "normal" experiences and family expectations can be subjected to judgment, criticism, or rejection. Your "normal" is lunacy in someone else's eyes and their "normal" is lunacy to you.

How in the world than, can one person judge another? If you haven't walked in another's shoes, if you haven't researched their disorder, if you know very little about the person than why do you deem yourself an expert in their affairs? As to judging others, how can we really do so? How do we know where the person comes from, what he/she went through? What kind of beliefs were instilled in this person? We judge others who are not like ourselves. We judge what we do not know. We condemn, criticize, and gossip about others who are outside our preconceived ideas of "fitting in". What makes your "normal" any better than the next persons? The person you are judging may be judging you.

We are raised to believe certain things, we are treated a certain way, we react, we think, we feel based on childhood experiences. For example, if you were consistently nagged at or yelled at as a child, chances are as an adult, friends and spouses nag you, yell at you, or treat you in a way that undermines the respect you deserve. Since you were not respected as a child, you do not know what it feels like to be respected and this carries forth into adulthood. To be disrespected is all you know. It is "normal" for you and so being disrespected happens again and again, year after year. You may be miserable about it, you may be sick of it, but you do not have a clue how to change it. We are not taught that there could be another way to think, feel, act, and behave.

I didn't question the way I felt, what I believed, or how I thought. This was me and that was it. Never did I consider that I could actually create healthy new brain pathways in order to act, feel, and think in a totally new way. I didn't know I could have a whole new set of beliefs. What an amazing discovery! We believe we are doomed the rest of our days with our beliefs and attitudes. "I'm hopeless. Nothing can help me. This is how I was born. It's no use even trying. I'm doomed."

Can you even try to imagine you do have choices? You aren't stuck or doomed after all. There is a way out. "We are who we are." But who, really, are we? Are we our beliefs, our feelings and emotions, our thoughts, our body? We are none of these. We are above and beyond whom and what we think we are. How do we achieve this knowledge of who we are? How do we get there? By unlearning who we are, by unraveling who we know ourselves to be. Where we make our mistake is the belief that we cannot change. "This is how I was born" or "This is how I was raised" are common statements. These statements are resistant statements, fear statements and what they really are saying is, "I don't want to change, I don't want to face myself, my pain, I would rather stay in the misery I know and cling to every day of my life."

Recognizing and learning what your "normal" is, is a huge leap forward in your self-discovery. Do not believe you cannot change any aspect of yourself. Do not be imprisoned by your "normal". Yes, it is all you have ever known, it is who you know yourself to be. Aren't you a wee bit curious though, to meet the true you, underneath all the junk heaped on you over the years?

Potpourri

♥ This whole process of getting to know you is an unlearning process, an undoing, a peeling of the layers. You cannot add anything to an already full body; you need to empty it first.

♥ As the negative goes down, the good goes up naturally. Forgiveness, compassion, non-judgment, patience, understanding, unconditional love, charity, acceptance, tolerance, etc. will increase as your negative needs decrease. You cannot **do** these things, you **are** these things and it cannot be forced. It's not a state of **doing**; it is a state of **being**. We need to rid ourselves of our false beliefs, perceptions, patterns, and behaviors in order for us to obtain higher levels of compassion, understanding, tolerance, patience, etc.

♥ There is, by no means, one answer to anything. One layer will always uncover another. "Well my mother was like such and such then so am I." That is the initial uncovering, but there is more beneath that initial realization, much more.

♥ There are false **needs** in us that cause us to **be** as we are. If we didn't have the need we wouldn't be that way. Find the source of your need: why you need to believe this or that, why you need to be treated the way you are, why you need drama, distress, sorrow, and dissatisfaction in your life. Find the source to set you free from your chains of false beliefs and false needs.

Do you allow people to walk all over you and let yourself be a doormat? Do you walk all over people? Where does this come from? What were you told or what did you witness that developed this false belief that in turn created an unhealthy need? Can you not hold a job or find one to your liking? Or did you flunk out of school or almost failed? Or are you an overachiever? Was it because you were told how stupid you are and that you will not amount to anything? Or was it because you were overly praised and complimented even when you didn't deserve it? Are you sweet, kind, and giving to everyone? What is the real reason for this? Is it truly from the goodness of your heart or is it a cover-up to a need you have to be this way? Are you being a people pleaser in order to get people to like you? Are you attention starved? Are you a control freak?

Can you start to see how getting to the source of your false needs will set you free in so many ways? Can you see that these unhealthy needs were created by false and unhealthy beliefs?

♥ In the beginning you may sabotage good that is getting close to you. Since you are not use to receiving pure good, it's scary and you push it away. You get sick, something breaks, you fight and the good backs off. All it takes is one time to allow this pure goodness into your life and the rest will start to flow. Oh there will be dams, lulls, and rapids along the way, but as you remove your obstacles and barriers, and as your awareness increases; you naturally allow the better to enter. Don't think because you did it once, than you have no more work to do; that you can rest on your laurels and sit back and do nothing. It doesn't work that way. Remember you are throwing out a lot of trash that has been stored inside you for years.

When you do receive the good in your life, remember it took a lot of courage and persistence to achieve this huge milestone! Though it may seem small to the external world, it is a huge advancement for your inner healing. Be aware that sometimes things get worse before they get better and this is where a lot of people stop and stall in their progress. "Oh, this isn't working, my life is worse because of it, not better." It's like a physical injury, it hurts worse before it improves; but that's how you know it is healing. Like how a cut itches as it starts to heal. The same applies in our internal work; the emotional and mental "nerves" need to come alive and heal for they have been severed years before. Take this as a sign that you are progressing.

♥ I use examples throughout the series for ease of clarification of certain concepts. For example if I am using a shopping addiction to present a concept and you are not a shopaholic than substitute it with your own addiction. Just because you are not a shopaholic doesn't mean the concept does not apply to you – it does. So substitute where you need to in order to make it your own; fill it in with your own situation. There are always opposites. Shy/brazen, give/take, gamble/cheap, emotional/non-emotional. When I give an example saying the person gives too little and you give too much then substitute your own circumstances since what I write applies to any given situation; insert giving too much where I state giving too little.

♥ If you are reading the topics and you say to yourself, "This doesn't apply to me – I don't treat myself that badly" think again. A seemingly innocent act of not doing something healthy for yourself is an indication that you are indeed imposing discomfort for yourself. Innocent acts like not taking supplements on a regular basis, little or no exercising, not eating as healthy as you could or not getting enough sleep. Some of this may stem from laziness which is a form of resistance or from the "busyness" you create in your life so as to not to feel your inner distress.

Perhaps you could ask yourself why you do not accomplish small simple healthy tasks for yourself. There are many unhealthy motives as to why we overeat: out of frustration, fear, protection, and self-hatred to name a few. This work, at times, calls for some hard truths to be recognized and acknowledged. It will not cause you to crumble but will heighten your awareness. You want to develop an unbiased look at yourself and the ways in which you treat yourself. Even the little things count.

♥ By no means think you need to become a "perfect" person.

Questions We Don't Ask Ourselves

I have found there are questions some of us do not ask ourselves; I know I didn't. I didn't even consider them because I didn't know they existed. Oh they may have passed through the brain fleetingly, but I did not delve deeper. "Why do I say the things I do? Why do I think the way I do? Why do I behave the way I do?"

For some, you take the life you were given and run with it - on auto pilot. There isn't a pause where we think that we can change our lives. We just go with what we have. Though we currently think, feel, and act in certain ways, it does not mean we are locked into this way of behavior; we have choices. We can choose to change our thinking, our beliefs...our entire mode of living.

We do not take notice of what we say, think or do. We do these automatically like breathing. Since we are programmed to do these things routinely we think these patterns are etched in stone.

"That's the way I am."
"I was raised this way."
"I was born this way."
"I like it just the way I am."
"I can't change, it's too hard."

"Better to stay with the devil you know."

"This is me, period!"

"A leopard can't change his spots." That may be true but you aren't a leopard. We put our thoughts, actions, and words on automatic. What you see is what you get, take it or leave it.

When we look at the universe, even just Earth, there is constant movement – birth, growth, change, renewal, death and creation. The process never stops. There is always motion and change. Something is being born and something is dying at every given moment. A blade of grass is growing somewhere. The air is in constant motion. The earth is spinning. Water is flowing. The sun always shines.

Our own body goes through constant change and renewal. It is in constant motion. Every part of our body from the skin to the molecular level is birthing, dying, and creating. So why can't our minds do the same? Why can't we apply this process of change and renewal to our way of thinking, of believing? We can, if we want to.

RUNNING AWAY FROM THE PAIN

For some of you, a little twinge of emotional pain will send you running for the hills in a panic. Got to get a drink, let's go shopping, time to gamble, pop a pill, or give me food!!! You will do anything not to feel one iota of emotional hurt. We run from emotional discomfort, but we quickly run to the doctor with physical pain. Either way, we don't want to feel the distress. For some of us, as we deal with our emotional hurts, our physical pain subsides also. We no longer need our physical pain as our need to hold onto emotional pain fades. Pain is an indication that something is certainly amiss; something is not right. Pain is scary and it freaking hurts!

There were times during my healing journey that I would do anything not to deal with processing hurtful and painful episodes. I would clean the house, go shopping, watch TV, talk on the phone; anything other than to feel the pain. After a few hours of detouring, I realized what I was doing. I was not facing past hurts. I was not allowing myself to heal through these feelings. It hurts. It's scary. I wasn't in the mood to feel the misery, but I knew if I didn't do the work, if I didn't feel, that I would rot by staying stagnant.

So with me kicking and screaming, cursing under my breath how unfair all this was, having my pity moment, I led myself back to my healing work. Talk about frustrating, aggravating, and wanting to scream my lungs out! I continued on my path. And I felt those feelings, and processed those memories. And afterward, once the layer of junk was released, there was such a sense of freedom, of renewal. I felt so much lighter, like a huge gob of gunk was removed from my inside. I felt renewed, free, and more of the real me emerged. The feeling of being released is indescribable, it feels that good!

If we run away from the pain it is because we are overwhelmed with emotion. We are in over our heads for the moment and need to step back and down. That is one reason why people stop so soon. They plunge into it head first, fast and furious, and are not properly prepared. Another reason we are overwhelmed is, we are releasing feelings and emotions that have been hidden within us for years. We are feeling them and acknowledging them for the first time. This is all so new and scary for us. At one point I felt like I was losing it – what I didn't realize was that I was overwhelmed with emotion. Once I learned that I may need to take a step back, and give myself a break, I no longer feared "losing it". You need to step back, and take a break. Go do something fun or something that you enjoy and that relaxes you. Try to do something healthy for yourself or forget healthy and go indulge in your favorite dessert.

It is crucial to distinguish when it is time to break, when it's time to push yourself, and when it is time to dig deep. It is very crucial for you to recognize when you may need professional help or you need to talk to a support group or individual. As you become more in tune with your body, you will know when to do what. Try the one foot at a time approach. Go slow, breathe, and stop when you have to. Remember that fear and resistance will be with you at all times and it is those times you need to push yourself through. Being overwhelmed with feeling and emotion is when you need to break and back off. You could break for an hour, a day, even a week or so.

As you calm yourself back, but you are still hesitant to continue on your healing path, then you need to ask yourself why. Is it because of fear and resistance, or because you are sick and tired of this work, or because deep inside you believe you do not deserve to heal? Perhaps you need professional help and feel uneasy about reaching out.

Whatever the reason, do not beat yourself up if you fall by the wayside. Every time we pick ourselves up, we are stronger than before. For some, the work will be grueling at times, but this is when we need to keep focused on the long term goal, and not the short term pain. Don't give up easily – you survived the incident, you will survive the memory.

Will the level of intensity be the same for everyone? No. Everyone has their own experiences of trauma, of dysfunction, of hurt and pain. Some of us were hurt unintentionally by well-meaning people; others were hurt by selfish people who were not concerned about our infant and childhood needs.

No matter what the intensity; feelings are feelings and they can be overwhelming for even the strongest of us. But we are in the process of handling, understanding, and controlling our feelings. In some aspects of my life I have overcome the emotional bondage and others are a work in progress.

There are two kinds of pain. The stagnant pain we are accustomed to and live with every day and there is productive pain, which heals us. The difference between productive pain and stagnant pain? You progress and heal with productive pain which is a temporary discomfort but it heals us whereas stagnant pain is life-lasting, permanent, and nonproductive. Stagnant pain is the pain we were raised with, it's our "normal". It is the misery within we unconsciously cling to. It eats away at you, slowly but surely, day by day, year by year.

WORDS

In all aspects of recovery work, it is important to use words that resonate with you, that calm you, that "fit" you. Words, when said aloud, should have a comforting feeling, a soothing effect. For example, perhaps the term "recovery work" does not sit well with you. You will feel it in your body somewhere that it doesn't blend, it irritates you in some way. Perhaps "my healing process" or "my transformation work" suits you better. Use words that work for you; your friend may use different words. Remember he/she has their journey and you have yours. Use a thesaurus which lists words of the same meaning and also opposite meanings.

It is important that you say the word aloud to feel its influence on the body. As an example, I was not fond of the term "letting it go" or "surrender and release". Perhaps these terms did not help me because after seeing them again and again, I still had no idea of how to "let it go". It left me frustrated. Using an online thesaurus, I came up with "leaving it behind" or "leave it behind". I could picture myself walking away, leaving it behind, and not looking back. When I say "Leave it behind" I feel the strength of its meaning. Experiment, play around, I was surprised at the difference a word could make, and still does in my healing.

Uneasiness in the body, from words, can come from the **sound** of the word or it can come from the **meaning** of the word or phrase. When the **sound** of the word distresses you, it is a signal to use a better suited word, one that harmonizes with your body instead of against it. When the **meaning**, the content, of the word or phrase distresses you, it is a signal that something is amiss within – a belief you hold as true could be actually untrue. The distress signals have different meanings; the sound of the word makes you uncomfortable whereas distress due to the meaning could be a clue concerning your inner state. "Leave it behind" gave me strength where "let it go" caused disinterest. It wasn't the words "I am safe" that woke me; it was the content of the phrase, its meaning. By discovering that I did not feel safe, it opened my eyes and led me to find out why.

When I started speaking affirmations, the list was a long one, and quite a few had "I am safe" in them. The first time I read out loud, "I am safe", my stomach churned like crazy. I was like, "What is this?" I said it again out loud, "I am safe." Again my stomach went into knots. I realized that I did not feel safe at all. It was a huge revelation for me. I did not ever consider if I felt safe or not. When I read the affirmations silently I did not have the same response. Sure, I felt weird and a little "out there" for saying affirmations out loud, but it was done in private, and I am grateful I overcame my uneasiness. From speaking out loud I discovered I was lacking a feeling of safety.

So, when you do read out loud, whether it be affirmations, passages from a book or song, or whatever source, notice how your body reacts. As you become aware of body messages, these feelings will get easier to detect. Tune in to your body, give it your attention. My stomach tells me, but we all have different areas; the chest, the head, an arm, it could even be in a finger or toe, but you will feel it. Does it feel smooth and comforted inside or does it feel jagged, alarmed, edgy, heavy, nervous, etc.? Then ask yourself if it is the sound of the word or is it the meaning of the word or phrase. If you think you won't be able to tell the difference, you will, trust yourself. Is it the sound that is causing uneasiness, or have you discovered something about yourself that needs to come to the surface in order to process and heal?

SECTION 2

SELF-STARTER HELPERS (MAKING THE DIG EASIER)

ACTIVITIES/MEDITATION/ YOGA/NUTRITION/ VISUALIZATION

It is crucial that you mingle your healing work with healthy outlets in order to relax, recharge, and to take your mind off the serious stuff and have some fun. Something as simple as walking does the mind and body good. Your nutritional intake and supplementation are other areas to consider.

Leisure activities, exercising, proper nutrition, visualization techniques, and meditation are but a few of the various healthy additions that will help you cope with everyday stress.

Exercise	Nature Walks
Hobbies	Photography
Puzzles	Dancing
Crafts	Writing
So many forms of meditation and yoga	Music: listening, attending, writing your own
Take classes	Volunteer
Reading	Seasonal Sports: baseball, skiing
Zone out TV – limited	Attending Art events: concerts, museums, ballet

Hiking	Dining out
Biking	Having a banana split without the guilt!

The list is almost endless of all the good things we can do for ourselves.

Becoming Self-Aware

The concept of "you are what you think" and that "your thoughts create your life" is far from new. These are ancient teachings that have been carried forth for millennium. And each generation has their own "New Age" teachers to continue these wisdoms. From the scholars in biblical times and ancient Eastern teachings to Ernest Holmes in the early 1900's to Emmet Fox in the 30's and 40's to Vernon Howard in the 60's and 70's to Louise Hay and Eckhart Tolle in the present day.

We have thousands of thoughts per day, how can we possibly know each and every one we think? We cannot, and is not the objective. The objective is to train yourself to become an observer of your thoughts. This is a most condensed explanation, but the key is to train yourself to watch your thoughts like you are watching a parade marching by. You are detached from your thoughts; no judging, no reacting, just watching.

Self-awareness will be discussed in detail throughout the guidebook series since it was and still is an integral part of my healing and recovery. It becomes a practice over time and starts to become a way of life. Enhancing your self-awareness includes becoming aware of your thoughts, your reactions, and your behaviors. This is a gradual process and doesn't happen overnight. It coincides with your healing and plays an important role in your self-renewal.

Let's look at self-awareness pertaining to our thoughts, behavior, insight, and compassion levels:

You are waiting in a checkout line, and the cashier is slow-moving.

1) Totally non self-aware:

> You comment to the cashier to hurry it along since your time is valuable. You mock the cashier as you talk to your friend on the cell phone, or
>
> You don't say anything to the cashier but you make your impatience known by your body language. As you leave the store you call her a name under your breathe.

2) A tiny bit self-aware:

> You comment to the cashier to hurry it along since you have places to go. In your frustration you help bag the groceries and you have no problem showing your annoyance. As you leave the store, a thought fleetingly passes through your brain that perhaps you were too hard on the cashier, but your mind immediately races elsewhere in thought.

3) A bit better:

> You try to exhibit patience, all the while steaming inside by the cashier's slowness, you put on a fake smile, and when you leave you think the person should be fired since they are so slow.

4) A bit more self-aware:

> You either verbally make a comment or display your annoyance with body language and are not friendly to the cashier. When you leave the store you realize how poorly you treated the person, but you make the cashier the bad person, it's their fault, not mine, "I'm not the slow one."

5) Getting there:

> Same as 4 but when you leave the store you ask yourself why the cashier annoyed you so much. "What did the cashier trigger within me, for me to get so annoyed?"

6) Getting better:

> In the process of showing your dissatisfaction you realize you are being unkind to the cashier and you immediately stop the behavior.

7) Almost there:

> As you are waiting in line, you observe the line moving slowly and notice the cashier is moving at a snail's pace. You have no judgment about the situation. You either pick up a magazine or you start saying affirmations; whatever you decide to use your time constructively.

8) There:

In addition to number 7, you observe strain on the cashier's face; it is obvious something is not right. While you are checking out you engage in conversation with the cashier and learn that this person just found out they have a medical condition, and she needs to keep working because she is a single mom with a 6 month old to feed. She apologizes for being so slow, but she is in shock from the bad medical report, but must keep working for the money. You just happen to know of a great clinic that helps people in her situation and you give her the name. The cashier smiles with gratitude since she didn't know where to turn. She expresses what a burden you have lifted off her shoulders. You made her day!

GRATITUDE

Deep-felt gratitude goes a long way for our everyday wellbeing. Be grateful for your job even if you hate it; give thanks for your car, your family, friends, the trees, the rain, and the neighbors. Learning to live in a state of gratitude will help to swipe away the nagging thoughts of what you do not have. I don't have a great house, I don't have a job, I want a new car, I want money, I want, I want, I want.

By being appreciative of what you already have opens the door for more to come in. You need to let go of your attachment to the results you seek. Let's say you want a new car and everyday it burns inside you that you don't have one and don't know how you will ever get one. You want that car no matter what. At this point, you are in complaint mode and feel sorry for me mode. When you are in this state you are not allowing yourself to receive what you do want. Instead you receive more of what you have which is no new car. If you begin to appreciate the car you already own and really <u>feel</u> thankful for your current car, situations will present itself to you to get a new car. For some, they will attract a car to them as if by magic, for others, money saving options and other answers will come to you. As long as you are in "I want it now" temper tantrum mode and are clinging to the outcome, a new car coming your way could take much longer or perhaps not at all.

During my healing process, which was intense at times, I still found it in my heart to thank my Creator. It kept me above water during those times as I was dealing with extreme opposites. On one hand, I was dealing with highly emotional and intense releasing of past trauma and on the other hand, I found comfort curling up underneath God's wing. Though I was swimming and nearly drowning in dark, swampy water, I also knew there was a Higher Power guiding me and that I would not drown since I placed my trust in His hands.

Find it in your heart during your day to thank All That Is for anything and everything, the good and the not so good. Be thankful for negative relationships in your life for they are trying to teach you something about yourself. Say thanks for getting that green light or that parking spot or the promotion or for finding the perfect mate. Be thankful for things that have not yet occurred. Be thankful for the long line of customers waiting for your goods or services, give thanks for the great new car that is coming your way; be thankful as if you already have it, for this is what sends it to you, a deep heartfelt gratitude for life.

As easy as it is focusing on what we do not have and feeling anger, resentment or jealousy, it is just as easy to focus on what we do have and to be grateful and appreciate what already exists in our lives.

HAPPINESS/JOY

Love is not something you do, it is something you are. Love loves through you on its own, you cannot force it to happen, it happens naturally like flowing water.

Happiness, joy, contentment, peace, love, compassion, and tolerance are internal states of being. They are not external reactions when something good happens to us, though we think they are. Happiness, joy, etc. are internal states of being which radiates out. They are not external states of living. You get excited or have a temporary thrill on the outside, but look at how external excitements abate rather quickly. You go to a party and have a blast…so much fun…the next day are you as excited as you were the night before while at the party? Chances are your pendulum swung back the other way, back to the seriousness of life. We can stop the pendulum of life and live in a state of contentment and peace no matter what is happening on the outside.

I am not saying we don't allow ourselves to have good times. What I am saying is we need to stop looking for happiness outside ourselves. We are so accustomed to living this way; we take it as the way it is supposed to be. You get a raise or a promotion, does this keep you thrilled for the rest of your days? The feelings wear off over time. This is what happens when you constantly seek gratification on the outside; a thrill here, an excitement there, all are very fleeting. We are like yo-yo's, up and down, up and down.

There is one aspect of life that keeps us tied to the pendulum of life. It is the life of opposites. Happy/sad, poor/rich, dark/light, male/female, abuser/victim, ill/well, in/out, love/fear, black/white, etc. Are we truly here to have a night of partying only to be in the dumps again the following morning? Or, are we here to rise above this illusion of polarities? There is a way out from a life of opposites; it is learning to live a life few of us knew even existed. This way of life exists, and is patiently awaiting our arrival.

LOVE OURSELVES/
ACCEPT OURSELVES

Learning how to love and accept yourself right now, with all your messes, mistakes, and regrets is crucial on the start of your yellow brick road tour. If you have told yourself how much you hate yourself than you can tell yourself how much you are willing to love yourself. A good place to start when you absolutely do not believe what you are saying is use the word "willing". Instead of saying, "I love myself", say instead, "I am willing to love myself" or "I am willing to learn to love myself." It makes a huge difference in helping to break down those inner brick walls you built around your heart.

To say "I love me" with absolutely no truth of emotion can lead to frustration and can stall forward movement. To say, "I am willing to love me" enables you to believe that such a miracle is possible, that indeed, you can end up loving yourself! Catch your thoughts when you start to berate yourself; this is how you open up to self-awareness, by becoming aware of how you think and what you tell yourself throughout the day. If you make a mistake, is that cause for you to totally hate yourself and berate yourself? Just say, "Okay I screwed up, that doesn't make me the worst person in the world. I still love and accept myself exactly as I am" or insert the word "willing" if need be.

For some of you, this will sound foreign and not in sync with your brain; it will feel like a foreign language. "What? Me? Be nice to myself?" Well, why not? Why not give it a go, stick with it, and see what happens. You may end up finding out you are not so bad after all!

And to those of you who are panicking right now about the thought of actually being nice to yourself, stop and take a breath. I know it goes against everything you have been taught about yourself; you are so ingrained with negative messages.

To go against "them" will cause you harm. If you are no longer with "them", then tell yourself that nothing bad will happen, that it is okay to like yourself. And, if you are still with "them" you are now an adult and no longer the child. Allow yourself to open up to new possibilities, be open to new ideas. Make the concept of loving yourself and accepting yourself into a reality; you owe it to yourself to do so.

To those who say, "But I already do love me!" we can always love ourselves more. Your external world is an indicator of how much self-love you actually do have. What is the condition of your: relationships, career, your treatment of yourself, how others treat you, how you treat others, your health, your wealth?

POSITIVE/HEALTHY
THINKING

Beneath our thoughts are the beliefs that fashion our views. When we get to the source of our beliefs, our thinking changes based on new knowledge acquired from discovering an unhealthy belief within. A slow and steady consistency helps to change a negative to a positive. When I first started practicing living in the present, not in the past or the future, but in the present, my brain hurt, so to speak! I could only do it for a quick moment before my focus would start to drift.

The same is true for thinking differently. It may "hurt" at first and you may only be able to think "positive" for a second or two, but little by little you will start to notice a change in your thinking. Let's say, you tell yourself over and over, "I have no luck. Bad luck is with me everywhere I go." We get hooked on saying the same thing over and over again. We do it automatically and subconsciously. We usually are not even aware of how often we tell ourselves negative suggestions.

So first, catch yourself saying it; that in itself is a huge step forward. Next you need to say something like, "No. Stop. I no longer need to believe bad luck is with me everywhere. Right now I do not know why I believe that, but where ever it came from it is wrong, all wrong." When you begin to change your thinking, there may be a tug of resistance because you do not want to give up your belief that bad luck is with you because it has become a part of you.

It is who you are; it makes you, you. You have been saying it for years. You can maintain your belief of bad luck and the attitude of "but that's who I am" or, you can find the source of this unhealthy belief and undo it, unlearn it, and instill a new belief of good luck. And that tiny tug of resistance? Just a tug is all it takes to keep you from your desire to change your thinking. And again you succumb to your unhealthy beliefs and another day passes of bad luck following you everywhere.

You feel as if you have no control over your thoughts, beliefs and behaviors, but you do – you need to unlearn and undo. If you truly want to stop telling yourself how unlucky you are, then you will stop telling yourself how unlucky you are.

If it were that easy and simple, why don't we change with a snap of the finger? There are layers that need to be uncovered, undone, overturned, rewired, and reprogrammed. Thinking is only the first part; just changing to a healthy way of thinking does wonders for you, but it doesn't eradicate the layers below that. The belief behind the statement needs to be discovered.

Let's say for every little flub or error you make, you tell yourself, "I can't believe I did that or How stupid am I." Before reading this guidebook, you had no idea you said that to yourself and now after reading this you are like, "Wow I say that all the time and didn't even know it." What a breakthrough! Once you know you are doing it, you go up a level in self-awareness and are able to begin the process of undoing this self-defeating behavior.

YOU CAN DO THIS/
PATIENCE WITH SELF

- Have the belief that you can do this even with all the doubt, fear, uncertainty, and self-hatred swirling around in your head.
- You have a choice, you can change.
- How you think can be changed.
- Effort, determination, courage, consistency, and the desire to heal will get you started.

"Rome wasn't built in a day" is true and true for you – you weren't built in a day either. With living in a world of "instant" everything today we lost touch of "patience being a virtue". Slow down with this; it isn't a race; it won't take forever. If you hop, skip and jump through it, you will probably end up needing to start over again. Who wants to do that?

You will fall along the way, you will go backwards at times, and you may not grasp some concepts the first time around. Temporarily, you may hate yourself, you may hate others, you will feel feelings and you will, at times, be drowning in a swamp of murky emotions. So what if you slip up, you fall, you go backwards, it is part of the process, it is part of the unlearning. You are doing something new for yourself. Is a violin master a master when he first picks up the violin?

What happens when you fall? Pick yourself back up, brush yourself off, grit your teeth at times, and get back on your healing path. Do not let one mistake, one movement backwards or one twinge of feeling tempt you to throw up your arms in disgust and tell yourself you can't do it. You can do it. You need not be alone through this; I discuss this topic, *Therapy/Support Systems* in the *Helpful Tools* section. No one is forcing you to do this work. You are doing it because you want to. You want a fulfilling life and you are willing to do the work regardless of all the fear and doubt within.

After suffering through setbacks, mistakes, oversights, the falling down to my knees, the intense release of emotion, the experience of feeling the feelings, I wouldn't trade it for the world. It set me free. I am so grateful I stuck with it because I freed myself from other people's dysfunctional beliefs that were instilled in me growing up. Their flaws, weaknesses, and unhealthy beliefs were eradicated from my brain.

The journey doesn't end; but the journey gets lighter, it grows ever wiser. You are elevated to higher levels of knowing, of understanding, of compassion, of being and the levels don't ever stop. You can go as high as you like. The path is not always dark and gloomy and emotional. Once the inner junk is released and gone for good, then the new and good and healthy can be fueled into your being. It's like coming out of a dark forest into a huge meadow where you can see clearly for miles around.

The best gift that came out of this was meeting me for the first time! I am still creating who I am, but I am me, more today than I ever was. Am I perfect? Not even close. Do my buttons still get pushed? Yup still dealing with issues. It is the way we handle them that changes, gained through our heightened awareness. It is our new way of thinking and knowing that changes old patterns.

SECTION 3

OBSTACLES AND BARRIERS (AS WE DIG)

ADDICTIONS

Addictions exist in many forms: sex, drugs, alcohol, shopping, eating, misery, receiving attention, being perfect, social media sites, the internet, television, exercise, romance novels, etc. We can have addictions to activities, feelings, states of mind, or emotions.

For me, an addiction is something you cannot live without on an obsessive level. It seems to control you instead of you controlling it (in the end though it doesn't control you, it only feels that way). It takes over and causes you to engage, even at times when you don't want to, but you must. You are a slave to the addiction. You feel depressed so you go shopping on an impulse.

If you can take it or leave it then you are not addicted. For example, back when you could smoke in bars, I had friends who only smoked when they went out drinking and even then they had one or two cigarettes. The question is though, can they not smoke when they go out drinking? Let's say you have a cocktail every night before dinner. If you don't have the cocktail, are you thinking about it, are you craving it, or are you not even thinking about it? Observing your level of attachment to an event, a feeling, or activity is a good indicator as to where you stand in terms of addiction.

What is interesting is how different addictions mask different symptoms. Addictions, obsessions and compulsions are all forms of symptom masking. They hide the real issues. They are cover-ups for internal pain and suffering – it is a form of temporary numbness. For instance, overeating hides fear of intimacy and the need for comfort. Smoking is a smokescreen covering up our fears, and giving us a false sense of courage. We are addicted to activities like gambling, to substances like drinking, to behaviors like fighting and arguing, to emotions like anger, or to our physical bodies like bulimia. And there are probably even more types than mentioned here.

We convince ourselves we cannot stop. When we truly want to stop an addiction we do. One reason we maintain our addictions is that we do not want to stop. We may not know how, or we don't know what to replace it with, or we are just not ready to give up our crutch. As long as that unfilled void exists within, another compulsion will take the place of the original addiction. We need to shift our focus away from the cover-up, and face the source of our addictions and compulsions, to finally rid the void that is ever with us.

The brain is moldable, we can rewire the brain from addiction. Addiction feeds our misery which has become an identifier of self for us. Misery is the basis of addiction, we are miserable about something. It hurts and we need to numb the pain. It provides only a temporary relief. We repeat the addiction over and over to gain relief, but no permanent relief has ever come out of an addiction. And for some of us, we don't even recognize that we are addicted to something, especially when it comes to feelings. We are in denial of our truth.

A common form of addiction is to our own misery, yet we are unaware this even exists. It is all we know; it is our "normal". That is why we are unaware. It has been with us since childhood and even infancy for some. There have been days I just wanted to hang onto my misery for dear life:

> "I do not want anyone taking away my dear old faithful misery; just let me wallow in my pain and

grief; let me pity myself to death, let me whine and groan the night away as to how unfair life is and it's all THEIR fault (whoever they are). It's so much easier living like this; dealing with what is familiar, and my life-long misery is very familiar and such a dear old adversary."

But hanging onto my lifelong misery only created another day of lifelong misery and another day and another year. I had to admit that I suffered with internal misery. Turning from negative to positive takes time, but it does work, and when you start to see it working, you only want more of it! And standing up to fear is an indescribable accomplishment. The saying "dealing with the devil you know" implies that another way of life will also include a "devil". See how hardwired we are, convinced that we will go from "the frying pan into the fire". It takes time, persistence and desire to think in new and healthy ways. I am not talking over the top Pollyanna positive.

What I mean is, if we can think negative (unhealthy), we can think positive (healthy). We need to unlearn and undo. People say, "If I think positive and what I want doesn't happen then I will be disappointed and upset. If I think negative and it doesn't happen, I already knew it was going to turn out badly anyway." Can you not see from this example how negative thinking affects our life?

The way we think is habitual. And habits can be broken.

Anxious Anticipation

Say you suffered ongoing trauma/abuse during childhood. It could be from your parents constantly arguing, or your siblings tormenting you, or some form of mental, physical, emotional, or sexual abuse. It can be any form of trauma/abuse including being ignored, neglected or abandoned. Ongoing abuse, for me, created a cycle of events. There were periods of rest, then anxious anticipation, then the trauma, then rest again. So life became a circle of: rest, anxious anticipation, trauma/abuse, rest. This happened repeatedly during my childhood.

We become adults, but this cycle of intensity is still with us. It is what we know, and so we need to reenact it ourselves.

We are in the calm stage – all is well.

> We do not get to stay here long – a silent anxious anticipation starts arising in us, the trauma is coming, we don't know when, the waiting is horrible. This is when cravings start to kick in and we need to self-abuse.

> We need to reenact the trauma in some way in order to quiet the anxiety. We eat a whole bag of potato chips, we gamble, steal, drink, shop, the list is endless. We do this in order to quiet down

the anxious anticipation screaming inside us. We abuse ourselves in some fashion. It could even be mentally beating ourselves up horribly. The potato chips or ice cream are gone, the abuse is over.

We feel worthless, guilty, shameful, but we calmed down the hidden monster inside of us…for now.

We are in the calm stage – all is well.

And the cycle repeats over and over nonstop until we consciously bring this to light and cease its hold on us.

BEATING YOURSELF UP

The first habit that needs work is "being your own worst enemy". The healing process is one where "two steps up, one step back" is commonplace and every time you take "one step back" or even two or three, it won't help one iota if you get down on yourself about it. This process, I have found, is like the ocean waves flowing in and flowing out. There is an ebb and flow to this process. At times, you will find yourself on a low side only to come back out of it higher and even more aware than before. We need to go "up and down" or "back and forth" or "in and out" with this process.

It is not like a frantic roller coaster ride of steep downward spirals and dizzying curves. The healing process is one of gradual, steady, upward progression. Part of the progression is moving backwards which allows you to gain strength and wisdom and this in turn, causes you to move further along on your path. When you move forward again, there is no need to step back again at this particular point of your path. You discovered what you needed to learn and allowed yourself to feel, remember, understand, and accept.

You will step back at times, but it's not back to the beginning. It will be a step back to the beginning of the level you are currently on or somewhere along that path. You do not step back to the levels you have already conquered. If you are going to beat yourself up every step of the way, than you must know it will hinder your healing journey.

Breaking the habit of beating yourself up is a great first step. Some of you are not even aware you do it. It is so ingrained that when you do make a mistake and call yourself an idiot or stupid or something worse, you do so naturally. You are not even aware you are calling yourself names or that you are criticizing yourself. Awareness is key. Next time you make a mistake or do something not up to your standards, stop and listen to what you tell yourself. Some of you may be surprised at what you hear swirling around in your head.

So, how to stop the noise? Like the rest of the obstacles and barriers, chances are high this stems from childhood conditioning and we continue that conditioning. It can seem so daunting to fix: "Why should I even bother, nothing will change, I am so stuck." Can you see in between the lines your internal misery at work? Why not try telling yourself something new. Something like:

> "I no longer need to beat myself up. This need to beat myself up came from unhealthy and false sources. I only belittle myself because others did or do it to me. It doesn't make it right and it doesn't make it true. It is far from true; it is wrong, it is a lie. I am willing to believe I am capable. I am willing to think a different way. I am willing to undo what was told me because I deserve to. I am a wonderful being who deserves to have the best in life and I now take the necessary steps to get there. I am willing to talk to me in positive, loving ways. I am willing to understand myself more and more and to change what isn't working and to enhance those things that are."

You deserve to rid the belief out of your head that "I'm a bad person."

BLAME

First and foremost, this guidebook series has no place for blame. We all are imperfect. We were raised by imperfect people, some worse than others. Some people were raised by well-meaning caregivers but they caused damage unintentionally, perhaps through limited parental skills. None of us are perfect; we carry forth what we learned as children. Does this make us all such bad terrible people; no. What is sad though is that we do not take the initiative to fix things in order for our lives and future generations to live a more fulfilling and functional life.

If a child was physically beaten, the chances he will beat his own children are 50/50. Let's say he doesn't beat his children but his unprocessed feelings from the beatings will appear somewhere in his/her adult life; whether the person suffers from depression, rage outbursts, addictions, unhealthy relationships, physical ailments, etc.

Fix what is broke and do not waste your time and energy on blaming parents, teachers, relatives, friends, authority figures, neighbors, schools, classmates, siblings, religious figures, etc. Your right to be angry may be justified, but we need to handle the anger in a controlled manner. It will be acknowledged, and it is necessary to release it and get it out of the body in order to heal. But that doesn't mean you are going to go hit old Mr. Jones over the head because when you were young, he use to scare you with his mean old dog, and now you have a fear of dogs.

This guidebook series is to get you started on your road to healing and recovery. If you are going to complain for hours on end, to anyone who will listen, how your husband did you wrong, this book is intended to gently guide you to the deeper issues at hand. It has to do with starting to see your patterns. To begin asking yourself why you need to be treated a certain way. Do not start blaming yourself and beating yourself up because you are not in a healthy, loving relationship. At your current level of understanding, how could you attract something you know very little about? You probably will attract what is familiar to you even if it isn't the healthiest of choices. At this state you have not acquired the additional knowledge and awareness needed.

So let's put blame to rest. We deserve a pity party for ourselves, a very brief one, and we do need to release our anger for the maltreatment. You will vent your anger, frustration, and hatred against those who did a less than satisfactory job in relating with you. **BUT**, and this is a big but; you will **NOT** physically harm, write, speak, seek revenge, or have contact with the person(s) who hurt you. If you currently communicate with the person because you live with them or whatever, you need to leave your inner work private for the moment. You are not to vent your feelings at the person(s) who hurt you during this stage of the process. Right now it is all about you and keeping the work where it belongs - with you.

If you live with the person, I can only imagine how difficult it might be to keep your mouth quiet especially when one is in the throes of sheer rage. That is why it is so crucial to read the guidebook series through first before you start working on yourself. You need to understand all the points involved in healing. If your rage or grieving issues are out of control or too overwhelming, you may need professional assistance in guiding you through. Do not hesitate to seek help when needed.

Some adults still operate, emotionally, on a child's level. We were not taught how to change and shift our perspectives emotionally as we age; we are not emotionally mature. It is a skill we need to learn. When someone overreacts to a situation, something triggered that person to go above and beyond a healthy mature adult response.

When we are processing emotions from childhood as an adult and are feeling them for the first time, it will be felt from the child's emotional level at first. We need to feel what we repressed all those years and the inner child needs to feel it first. Though we are feeling through the child's heart, we are doing it from an adult perspective.

Before we can talk to anyone who has hurt us, we first need to expel those long lost emotions and process them which will free you from the experience. The memories will not leave, but you will no longer be bound by them. You control the memories; the memories no longer control you.

One indication that you have finished processing a memory is when you can discuss it without becoming overly reactive and emotional. I'm not saying a few tears may appear, that's fine, but if you are still reacting violently or are overly emotional than you have not fully processed the event. You are not ready or qualified to speak with the person who hurt you. Let's look at it from this angle:

1) You remember a traumatic incident as a child and the person who hurt you was very close to you.
2) You are in the process of releasing: denial, shock denial, shock, realization, grief, anger, memory detachment

3) During the anger stage you go and rage at the person who hurt you, or during the grief stage you go and cry to the person.

4) So you vented. So now what? How long did it make you feel good? 5 minutes? One hour? And what benefit did you derive from screaming or crying at this person? What true lasting benefit came out of the screaming or crying match for you personally? Maybe a temporary release of rage that could have been released at the gym, or through writing or confiding in a trusted friend or professional.

What do you want from this person, a heartfelt apology, for them to get on their knees and beg for your forgiveness? You want them to know that you know? These are all legitimate wants on your part, but wouldn't you rather be in a better informed, emotionally mature position before you approach the person who hurt you? It can be very therapeutic to approach the person and discuss your side of the situation; but that should happen when you achieve emotional maturity and have processed your feelings. At this stage, it may end up a disaster for you.

At this point in time you cannot express how you feel, so how can you express to the very person who hurt you? You want to be in a position when you do talk to the person, that in the end, you not only survived but you thrived and their dysfunctional ways did not destroy you. You also need to come from a mature position; to be able to talk with this person without "losing it" in any way. To say what you need to say in order for you to heal and not have any expectations of the person's reaction.

The reason you are speaking with this person is for your healing; it is not for you to receive anything back from this person such as an apology or confession. That is only an added benefit. If you are looking for a specific outcome from the person who hurt you, you may be in for a shocking surprise. You must be prepared that the person may not give you what you want; you may get the exact opposite. At this point, are you prepared for that? Why at this stage would you want to do that to yourself? You have enough on your plate that you are sorting through, why add a possible rejection or denial or a total disregard for your needs at this moment? Do you really think you are in a position to take that on? Are you emotionally mature and stable to face it? Do you really want to? You have better things to do right now than to set yourself up for a fall. You will get your turn, and when you do, you will be a winner and not a victim. Patience is required.

And to those of you who went and vented, I truly hope the outcome was in your favor. If not, then continue on, rack it up to experience, and know that in the future, when you are in a better place emotionally and mentally, than you can consider addressing the person. You may have been devastated by the reaction you received and were very hurt. Just know, it needn't be this way, it doesn't have to hurt forever. If the people who hurt you have passed on, though you cannot see them, you can release your feelings about them through writing and talking.

One exercise to practice is to notice how often we blame others for our misfortunes. Notice when a friend speaks about her marriage how she blames the husband for everything. Instead, she could be asking herself why she does she need to be treated the way she is. The exercise is to divert your attention away from the other party and concentrate on yourself. It is much easier to blame the other, to want that person to change and not you. To mold that person into the person you want he/she to be. Then you will be happy? What if the person changed for you and did everything you wanted. Do you think all your internal misery is going to just vanish because you now have a robot to please you? Your misery is where you left it, inside festering away.

At times, I would just groan that I wanted to blame the world instead of doing the work. That was so much easier, but nothing got done. I gave all my power away by blaming others. I was remaining stuck and was having a pity party. In the end, that was not what I wanted. So again and again I refocused the work back to me. Over time, I felt empowered. I felt like I was a person who deserved to be fixed and the only one to do that for me, was me.

For those of you who blame themselves for everything that is wrong, was wrong and will be wrong, start to see the martyr behavior within. Are you sacrificing your own well-being in order to uphold some religious or caretaker dictate? "It is my entire fault. I have no one to blame but me. I must suffer for my indiscretions, my sins, my whatever." You were not put on this earth to carry the world's burdens on your shoulders.

Overreactions are symptoms for something deeper going on. Be curious; seek to discover what lies within. Get your power back, stop giving it away by blaming others or yourself. Take control of your life; it is your life. Do you really want to keep giving it away?

CONTROL

How many of us love to control, to feel that air of superiority? How many of us hate to control, and want others to control us? How many of us like both, domination and submission? There are people who want to control everything: their friends, spouses, children, finances, everything and everyone. Some do it harshly, others do it oh so sweetly…but it still comes down to the need to be superior. Then there are those who need to be told to do anything and everything, their level of feeling inferior runs deep. Then you have people who control, and then they want to be controlled and dominated, from superior to inferior.

The above control needs will be addressed as we go through the healing process, but for now, the focus is on issues that surface daily in our lives. Simply put, any stress we experience is because the situation did not go our way. We fight the outcome instead of accepting what life hands us. Of all the traits we cling to, I think control is one of the strongest. Why shouldn't we want things to go our way? After all, "It's my life, I want it my way." Then there are those who demand they come first, "It's mine and I want it. It's my way or the highway." And others, "Of course it didn't go my way, it never does."

This overwhelming need to have things go our way could be a reflection of how we didn't get our way when younger. How you were not listened to or acknowledged during your formative years.

Another reason for control may be to keep people away from us; we fear being "found out" and people won't like us or they will mock and judge us. They will see us for the coward we are. People will see our insecurities.

We get upset when things do not go our way; we do not accept what happened. Instead we focus on our dismay. This is where acceptance plays a huge part. We fume inside and for some, feelings of rejection surface as well as not feeling worthy. We are angry we did not get what we wanted. We are depressed because we feel rejected, and we hate ourselves because we feel unworthy. Our relentless need to be right, our persistent need to have it our way, our deep quest to control our situations is a big player in the field of obstacles and barriers. We think we are in control when actually control is controlling us!

Control lives our lives. That long line in the supermarket, we feel impatience or frustration inside. We feel that way because we want no lines, we want it our way. Someone doesn't respond or react the way we want them to, so we get angry or hurt or put off. Why? Because we wanted a certain response, again, control. It's everywhere, in everything we do, think, and act. We unknowingly, or knowingly, try to control other people, the weather, the traffic, people's thoughts, and on and on.

How great would it be if we just let life happen? We accept all that is given us - long lines, traffic, daily challenges. Learning to use delays as times to meditate, say affirmations and pray is a boost to your inner peace. Letting people and life be themselves without expectation. Letting go and letting life happen. Allowing a Higher Power to direct your life, and to let this Power steer the ship and guide you into harmonious relationships, financial abundance and a healthy body.

How do we even begin to start shifting our gears into another way of thinking? How do we let go and let life happen? As you unleash yourself to the past emotionally, as your unconscious, unhealthy states of belief rise to the surface, it washes away not just the negative feeling, but it increases your awareness and insight of the positive qualities: compassion, understanding and knowing. As the negative goes down, the positive naturally rises. Your ability to accept more and more of life's situations increase as you unlearn your life.

DEFENDING THE PERSON(S) WHO HURT YOU

Who doesn't want to believe that their life growing up was just fine? In some areas, it probably was. What about where it wasn't so fine? Those darker places growing up. The behind the door secrets that the outside world did not see? It gets buried deep within our psyche and our body only to emerge in our adult lives as emotional, mental or physical ailments.

When these dark places are bought up and out, we may defend them, we may justify them, and we may make excuses. We make it seem right in our minds. We have fear of being rejected or criticized by society if they knew the truth. We make less than desirable circumstances plausible. We want to believe our lives growing up were normal and healthy.

I defended my primary abuser at first and was doing so unconsciously. It was bought to my attention that I was defending the very person who abused me. Perhaps we defend our dark past because we do not want to admit the truth. We want to avoid feelings and emotions that hurt us, scare us, and scarred us.

"There was nothing wrong with me growing up, it was great, and everyone was great. The past is over, what's done is done." Is it done? Is it ever really done? Unfortunately, no, not until we face it. Do you think all the hurt, pain, trauma, and suffering you endured as a child and/or infant just magically left? Just left your mind and body like it didn't happen? That would be great if it happened that way, but it doesn't. It stays with us until we release it.

So do we want these darker places to keep hurting us, or do we want to take control of them? Our unresolved thoughts, feelings and emotions will stay unresolved, until we decide to do something about them. It is so easy to bury our heads in denial, to move forward and not look back. But are you really moving forward?

"Who in their right mind wants to go through that again? Not I, no thank you – once was enough. I will take the misery that I live with day in and day out." Realize that the internal misery you live with every day is stagnant; non-productive. It is subtle, at times, but it is there. It is unacknowledged, unexpressed feelings from long ago. It keeps you stuck in your endless circle of pain. You ignore your internal pain every day hoping that one day it will go away on its own. Well it won't.

Perhaps you do want to release all the gunk inside, but do not know where to start. This is why I am writing the guidebook series. To help show you a way to get you started on your healing journey. Now we are adults, so what do we do about the dark places growing up? We defend and excuse them away. We keep them well hidden and buried deep. "That's how it was in my generation. My parents only did the best they could. That's how life was back then." And it is true, your parents/guardians did the best they knew. Of course if they knew different they would have done different. But that is no excuse to ignore how we *felt* at the time. And that is what needs to be recognized and acknowledged. How we *felt*. What matters is how you processed the pain at the time. Chances are these thoughts, feelings and emotions were not verbally expressed or understood by our child mind.

This healing process is not about blaming others. It is about recognizing, acknowledging, and releasing feelings and thoughts we endured during painful periods of infancy/childhood. This is what we need to do, to look at the source of our pain. Where do you think your internal misery came from? It came from unhealthy, incorrect, misdirected mindsets. That was my incentive to change. I did not want other people's negative beliefs to keep controlling my adult life. I needed to get rid of all the false, unhealthy beliefs instilled in me as an infant/child.

"Oh please, who wants to go back there – to childhood, it's over and done." But it isn't over and done. It is one cause of your daily internal misery. The other cause is lack of living as a being. We are human beings, but we tend to live mostly as humans.

How many of us cast our internal misery onto others through anger and fighting, criticism, humiliation, silence, using people, being selfish, and manipulating, to name a few? And how many of us cast our internal misery onto ourselves through addictions, depression, and disregard for oneself? How many of us lack self-love, self-worth, and self-respect? We feed our internal misery through external means to keep the cycle going. We do not want to fix what is broke, because many of us don't even realize how broken we truly are. We would rather numb the pain through medication, addictions, etc.

Do you truly want to keep living with a non-productive, stagnant pain? Or, do you want to gather up the strength and courage to face reality? The pain you live with every day is stagnant, non-productive. Healing pain is forward movement, it brings you to a new level of thinking, of being, and of having.

We defend our childhood, parents, guardians, siblings, environment, schools and teachers, our beliefs, and ourselves. We will do anything not to face the past. But in the end, who are you hurting? Only yourself by staying in denial. If your father habitually beat you, don't you think you have the right to *feel* the pain he inflicted upon you both physically and mentally? And don't you think you have the right to heal from that pain? To no longer be bound to the damage done to you? To release that pain for good. In order for you to heal you need to stop defending the people who hurt you. Like you, they made mistakes, they did things wrong, whether it was done consciously or unconsciously.

What matters is setting yourself straight by undoing the wrongs done to you, whether they were done to you on purpose or by ignorance. Not all parents are horrible people, far from it. This is not about right or wrong, good or bad. It is about showing you that you do have alternatives and you can improve your life. You can undo what happened to you. Most of all you deserve to live a life of your own making. It is of your own creation, and not a life based upon others and their incorrect/unhealthy ways.

I am not saying to never speak with these people again, or to hate them with a passion. What I am saying is that you need to stop defending them in order to concentrate on you and getting yourself better. By focusing on the people who hurt you, it takes your attention away from your feelings and your healing.

DENIAL & REPRESSION

> "How do we know we are in
> denial, if we are in denial?"
> Virginia Anne

Denial is repressed knowledge we have about circumstances, ourselves, and others. It causes us to be blind to the facts. Denial is when we refuse to accept the truth. It keeps us from feeling what we need to feel, seeing what we need to see, and doing what needs to be done.

Denial of your real childhood, your current conditions, and yourself are just a sampling of where denial can reign in your life. How many people do you know that "stick their head in the sand"? When asked about my childhood, I would tell people how great it was growing up as a kid. We were always outside playing. We belonged to a country club that had day camp in the summer with an Olympic sized swimming pool. There were 1st place swimming trophies, picnics and parties, ice skating and sleigh riding in the winter. I went to Halloween and Christmas parties every year at the local firehouse. Patches on our pant legs where the knees wore out, mud pies, bicycles, the game of tag, and hide-n-go seek with the neighborhood kids. In this regard, life for me was great and I loved it.

When you look at my childhood description, do you see where all of this was external happenings? What about behind closed doors? Where is there mention of the family unit and the side not shown to the public eye? We all were raised behind closed doors. I had repressed and denied what went on behind those doors until events forced me to finally open them. I needed to see, feel, and experience events I had repressed long ago.

Denial is a coping mechanism. We bury things in order not to feel the pain or fear. Memories don't ever go away, we bury them. We shove them deep down somewhere but they are still within us. They are lodged in our brains and bodies. These memories, beliefs, thoughts, feelings, and behaviors shape and mold us into the adults we are today.

There is no question that denial and repression wreak havoc on your psyche, your mental well-being, and your quality of life. It pushes up and out through addictions, negative behaviors, illness, unhealthy situations, depression, and a myriad of other thought processes and external situations. Denial wants to be known; it wants to be freed, so the body can begin the healing process both mentally and physically. How many people do you know, including yourself that say some of the following?

- His girlfriend treats him like garbage, uses him for her own desires, and if asked if he loves himself will say, "Of course I love myself."
- "I had great parents." (When they were around to care for us).
- "I'm not jealous." (I just think that person doesn't deserve such a big house.)
- "I'm not greedy, I give all the time." (But only when it suits you to do so).
- "Hey, my parents beat me, that's why I am the way I am."

- The "know-it-all" attitude, the "nothing bothers me" stance, the "I am tough and strong" mentality and the "I don't need anyone" attitude.
- "There is nothing wrong with me; it's all their fault. Not my problem they can't see my point of view."
- Someone is struck with a medical condition and does not know to link it to past conditioning. "I don't have a problem. Why go back? The past is the past, it's over."
- "I'm not the one with the problem, they are the one with the problem."
- "Everything is wonderful. I am wonderful, the house is wonderful, and my spouse and job are wonderful." (But you know otherwise).
- How someone depicts their life on social media and it does not match the reality of their situation. (Lots of denial).

We keep things down and hidden. The wife knows she is in a horrendous marriage, but is too fearful to face it. Where would she go? How would she live? Her image of a happy home would be destroyed. So she pretends all is well and denies, denies, denies. She is miserable because of it and so creates a fantasy life on social media. And she starts believing her life is just like her computer life; but it isn't.

Another possible form of denial is when someone verbalizes a comment, observation, etc. to you concerning your appearance, your manner, or whatever and you have trouble accepting it. Some of us immediately react defensively and deny what is being said. Some of us become quiet and don't say a word thinking that what this person said must be true because why else would he/she say it? Perhaps some of you get angry inside but do not say a word.

When someone shares their observation of you, before you react, observe how the comment or criticism was delivered. Did the person deliver it in a harsh, abusive, non-feeling way? Or was it kind and caring? Did the person believe by saying something to you that it would help you in some way? Or was the person lashing out at you?

People say things out of anger, jealousy, or revenge. They do not accept you the way you are, and are trying to mold you to suit their needs. Or they do it because they care for your well-being. So perhaps it wasn't said in the best way possible, but after observing who said it and the possible reasons why, let's assume they did it because they care for you. And let's say your first reaction is a defensive stance. You deny it and walk away. When you are by yourself and with no one knowing, evaluate what the person said. As hard as it may be, was there a kernel of truth to what was said? Is it possible the person is speaking the truth? If so, what will you do about it? Stay in denial or get to the bottom of the behavior so it doesn't control you anymore? As always you have a choice. If you strongly believe the person said it because of their own shortcomings then dismiss what was said and know it is their problem not yours.

How can we be in denial when we don't know that we are in denial? There are stages in the healing process and the first stage is denial. As you allow yourself to open up to what's inside, the denial will transform into a conscious knowing, so you can process it and be rid of it. As we progress and look back to see how far we have come, we then see where we were in denial.

Acknowledgment is breaking through the barrier of denial and repression. Acknowledging feelings, emotions, beliefs, and behaviors, for some, will initiate instant change. It's because you feel it, as well as know it. For others, you will know it, but not feel it, and so change is not initiated. Acknowledging brings up what must be released. It releases it from being buried within and raises it into your consciousness. Admitting some hard truths to yourself is another step closer to releasing it for good. You are on your way!

You may not want to deal with something at the moment, but at least you acknowledge it exists; you no longer deny its existence. Instead of repressing the pain, you now tell yourself, "I have this pain or issue or trait or whatever. Right now I cannot deal with it, but I will at a later date. I am not repressing it, I know it exists; there is no reason for me to repress it anymore."

EXISTING BELIEFS

Are you willing to take an honest look at your beliefs? Can you be open that maybe some of your beliefs are faulty, unhealthy, or totally wrong? This doesn't happen at once; it happens gradually. Will some realizations come to you in a flash, the answer is yes. Will other conditions stick to you like super glue? Yes to that also. But, overall, this process is a gradual, forward steady progression. Even on the days when you take two steps back, you are still progressing for when you start in forward motion again you are further along than before.

The beliefs we hold close to us today were formed in our early years. For example, if you were raised that this sports team is the absolute best, then chances are you will believe that as an adult. You have been exposed to this team for a long period of time and so have a belief that they are the best. I am using a benign example here, and there is nothing wrong with having a favorite team. Then there are those who go opposite of what you were exposed to. You may come to hate the team that your caretaker liked, as a means to express your individuality. Also, if there is animosity towards the person, then you may do the opposite of their likes.

When I was through processing memories of past trauma, I thought I was done and free and everything was wonderful. Or so I thought. What lay before me was a pile of beliefs that no longer worked for me. Many of my beliefs, thoughts, behaviors, emotions, feelings, perceptions, and attitudes were all based on untruths. Almost everything I thought to be true was untrue. My beliefs were faulty and were instilled in me by unhealthy, selfish people. My beliefs about money, relationships, intimacy, love, and life were all skewed. But the most damaging beliefs I held were the ones that I believed about myself.

I had deep-seated beliefs that I did not deserve good. That I was unworthy of harmonious relationships, health and wealth. I was angry that I had to fix what other people caused; because of them my life got twisted. So what to do? Scream and yell at them for all the wrong they did to me? What would the screaming get me; a minute, a day of satisfaction? I wanted something that was permanent; that would last and I was not interested in including those that hurt me. This was about me and fixing me and changing me. And it made sense that my thinking, beliefs, attitudes, and behaviors would be a mess since parts of my upbringing were a mess.

So I picked up a hammer and chisel and started chipping away; little by little. Some of the chipping away included: writing my feelings, professional therapy, reading about specific conditions that pertained to me (co-dependent tendencies for one), affirmations, and my continuing journey learning about my Higher Power which I call God. This chipping away included undoing what was done, and infusing new, healthy brain pathways after the junk was released.

Do not walk around or over your obstacles. You will find yourself facing the same pile again and again. As you start chipping away, you develop the desire and determination to rid yourself of your faulty belief system. I wanted to rid myself of other's thoughts, beliefs and behaviors that shaped me into who I was. I wanted to create me. I wanted to thrive and live with my own creation; one of self-love, dignity, self-respect and integrity to name a few.

Did I eventually clear my path so I could continue walking along my road of healing; yes I did. Did some of these beliefs come forward with me - of course. Some beliefs were easy to get rid of and replaced, while others took time. Even though some boulders were destroyed, I still had pebbles of beliefs I knew needed working on. I put those in my pocket and marched forward knowing I would tend to them along the way. There were also beliefs that were super glued within me, and these would take extra time and care. All my beliefs were not resolved at once, and that's okay. I am referring to false and unhealthy beliefs. My beliefs that held true and good remained with me.

A note to those that think all this work for yourself is selfish and that others come first. Ask yourself who told you that? Someone that wanted their needs met without considering yours? Or does it come from a religious background where God and others come first before oneself? I believe that the Divine does come first, but don't you think your Creator wants you to love yourself also? And if you were not taught how to love yourself, don't you think this powerful Being wants you to learn? And just because you are working on yourself doesn't mean you are putting the Divine in the back seat. You learned lots of things over the years; now you are learning a new thing. You are learning about you and it is the best subject you will ever teach yourself! So rid yourself of the belief that this work is selfish. That's a belief that needs fixing!

FEAR

I can guarantee this: fear and resistance will be with you every step of the way. Is this cause to throw up your hands and say, "Why bother?" No it isn't cause for you to walk away. You now have the upper hand, you know what's coming and can be ready for it. In the beginning, fear and resistance will win out from time to time. If you give up early on, it could be due to fear of having to feel. Of having to come out of denial. To see things you do not want to see. No one can force you to do this work, but before you run away, ask yourself:

> "What is it that I am so afraid of?"
>
> "Do I have what it takes to keep moving forward despite the fear?"
>
> "Do I do it afraid?"
>
> "Am I ready?"
>
> "I know all this junk inside me will come out in some form or the other if I don't handle it. Is illness and constant misery what I truly want to call my life?"
>
> "Do I want to keep living with unhealthy relationships, situations, addictions and thought patterns?"

"Am I willing to believe I can do this despite the pain and the fear?"
"Am I willing to overcome my fear of fear and do what is truly best for me?"
"Do I want to love me on a deep level before I die?"

If you find yourself not ready, then you aren't. It doesn't make you a bad person, a wrong person, or a weak person. It just makes you a person who isn't ready and there is nothing wrong with that. I am not ready to do certain things yet, but I don't condemn myself for it; I accept it. And whatever you do, don't fall into the pattern of beating yourself up, or feeling guilt and/or shame. Be proud that you know yourself well enough to make this decision.

Changes that you are willing to make can create resistance and fear; any change comes with fear, even good ones. Our world of opposites create fear: Fear of failure, fear of success, fear of losing control, fear of being in control, fear of the unknown, fear of the known, fear of abandonment, fear of being emotionally smothered, fear of loneliness, fear of too many people, fear of losing others, fear of others staying, fear of what you may remember, fear of not remembering, fear of what the family will think, fear of what the family will do. Without opposites, and living in the neutral is another ultimate goal of recovery. But, for now, getting back to fear, it controls us, paralyzes us, keeps us in unhealthy situations, and keeps us stagnant.

Do I have fears to overcome? Of course I do; it is a matter of priorities. Which fears are important to you and which ones do you want to tackle? It lives and breathes within us on many levels, in many different areas, and in many different ways. We bury it deeply and disguise it. We do not recognize it as fear and we are in denial of it. "Who me, afraid? No way" you say as you try to convince yourself and others what a brave soul you are.

We disguise our fear when we are being brash, arrogant, and haughty. We disguise it by being a comedian, being silent, and by conducting ourselves in an overly confident manner. We are raised to believe that having fear is a weakness and a flaw. To possess fear is to be regarded as a weak individual, a coward. So we deny it and bury it. Instead we eat a ½ gallon of ice cream, or drink a six-pack of beer, go on a shopping spree, clean the house, have random sex, start a fight, stay in horrendous situations, live in a state of numbness, or be a couch potato. We will do almost anything other than to confront our fear and learn to live and work with it.

Ask yourself what alternate behavior you engage in to avoid your fear of your fear. Yes, we are absolutely terrified of our fears. They scare the daylights out of us, we run as fast as we can and as far away as we can from the terror of fear. Whether the running comes in the form of staring at the bottom of an empty liquor bottle or maxing out your credit cards; we will keep running until we say enough is enough. The sooner we can admit to our fear, to acknowledge to ourselves that we do have fear and a lot of it, the sooner we can start to conquer it. We allow it to control us and manipulate us in ways we do not even realize.

Accept fear and resistance as a catalyst to change. As you face your fear head on and you walk right past resistance, your world will experience a shift. As you learn to face the fear and resistance, you will find yourself gaining power over your inner self. You start to become the real you, and not this made up person someone else created.

Fear and resistance begins to lose its hold on you the further you progress on your journey. You are able to conquer your fears and to control them. They no longer control you. And when fear and resistance surfaces, you will be at a place where it won't destroy you. You will see them as they are – catalysts for change – enforcers pushing you to become your best.

Guilt/Shame

Guilt, for the purposes of this guidebook series, means you feel guilty "going against" your caretakers, your beliefs, and anything else that creates guilt within. "How dare you go against the family unit" you hear your inner voice screaming. You need to know that you are not going against anything or anyone. Doing this work has nothing to do with that.

This work is to heal you, to help give you the life you deserve. This work is allowing your voice to be heard for the first time. To allow your emotions to be felt. To create an internal way of living that wasn't taught to you during your most crucial years of growth. You are fixing what another's inadequacies did to you. To be rid of their mistaken beliefs that were instilled in them as children and were passed to you. You are breaking a vicious cycle. And again, this is not about blame, this is about fixing, correcting, making new. This book is not about how Aunt Betsy treated you; it's about what you thought and how you felt the way Aunt Betsy treated you.

There are those who produce they own guilt by hurting others as a way of hurting themselves. This is self-imposed guilt. People add more and more guilt to their lives. Self-imposed guilt stems from guilt being thrown at you during your younger years.

What guilt do you live with? Is your guilt self-imposed or from external factors? Decide whether you want to continue being a certain way or changing an aspect of yourself into something loving and worthwhile. There may be other guilt scenarios I haven't touched upon, so be sure to incorporate your "guilt trip" into your healing so you can be free of it.

For those of you who were raised with guilt as a disciplinary tool whether by caretakers, schools, religions, or whomever, you deserve to rid yourself of such guilt. It was used in order to control you. And along with the guilt comes shame and fear; lots of fear. Your tendency to feel unfounded guilt and shame will diminish as your awareness increases. To seek ways to rid yourself of this ingrained control tactic is one of the best gifts you can give yourself.

All this applies to shame as well. To be raised feeling ashamed of anything you do or say becomes a life of self-doubt, hesitancy, decision-making inadequacies, or little or no self-esteem, and the list goes on and on. Being made to feel shame through coercion could be one reason why you are reading this guidebook series, to finally rid yourself of other's inadequate ways of teaching whether they be: parents, teachers, relatives, friends, authority figures, neighbors, schools, classmates, siblings, religious figures, etc.

Habits (Unhealthy Habits)

A habit is a long-term practice.

A habit is a form of addiction.

We create a dependence on the habit. We think we cannot live without it.

We become fixated on the pattern. We think and think about our unhealthy habit(s).

We are impulsive because of our addiction to the habit.

We are obsessed with the practice.

We allow the habit to control us.

We are accustomed to the habit; it becomes a way of life for us.

It gets ingrained within us.

We cling to the habit out of desperation for satisfaction.

We attach ourselves to it; we are the barnacle, we are not the habit.

We let it grow a deep tap root within us.

The pattern eventually puts us in a rut.

An unhealthy habit is a form of self-punishment.

A habit gives a fleeting satisfaction which is why we do the habit over and over again.

It is a false satisfaction; we are using the habit trying to fill a void within us.

We erroneously think habits will take away our pain, that it will make us feel better. It only numbs us temporarily and then the cycle starts again. We are a slave to it. We hate it, but feel powerless over it.

Some reasons a habit may develop are: we do not want to look at ourselves, or face painful realities, or to feel painful emotions.

A habit can develop from having unmet needs as a child. You did not receive what was needed during various stages of your growth.

There are various forms of habits. Habits are not all physical actions, i.e. shopping compulsion, eating disorders, etc. We develop habits of:

Worrying
Gossiping
Judging others
There are as many mental habits as there are physical ones.

Some habits get passed down from one generation to the next. For example, if dinner was served at 6 pm than chances are good you will eat dinner at 6 pm even after you leave and go out on your own.

Habits can come from:

Unmet needs
A learned behavior

Made scared as a child (If you don't do this, I will call the police on you).

Mocked as a child

Fear can become a habit and is the most devastating, debilitating one.

We can:

Dissolve the habit
Break a habit
Accept the habit
Acknowledge the habit
Leave behind the habit
Let it go
Face the habit
Get rid of the habit
Do away with the habit
Stop the habit
Replace the habit
There are as many ways as dissolving a habit as there are habits.

Habits, phobias, compulsions, obsessions, addictions, for me, overlap, intertwine, are related and have much in common. Covering these important components is outside the scope of this guidebook; I present them here for awareness purposes. You may find yourself though, on your healing path, giving up habits and addictions that no longer serve you as your awareness levels increase.

IDENTITY

Since conception we have an identity label attached to us that describes us. We are the baby. We may be a colicky baby or a quiet baby. We are the toddler - either a well-behaved one or not. As pre-teens we can be moody, grouchy or a great kid. We have an identity label and we have an adjective to that label. She/he is a homemaker, a company president, an employee, or a student. She/he is good/bad, poor/wealthy, smart/dumb, or married/single.

What happens is we associate ourselves with our identity. We think we are that label. I am wealthy is not who you are, it is something you have acquired. I am an astronaut. That is not who you are, it is what you do. Though we are labeled with an identity and descriptions to support that identity, we are not the label. It may be what we do, what we have acquired or what we have accomplished.

You then ask, "Well what or who am I then?" On ground levels of human existence, polarities (opposites) exist all around us. Smart/dumb, married/single. We can go in/out, up/down, or back/forth. We have black/white, yes/no, love/fear, peace/chaos, knowing/non-knowing. It may be hard for some to imagine a world without polarities or time or space. But it does exist. That is the "being" side of who we are. We as beings don't "live" here on earth like our human side. Our being side is timeless, dimensionless, and pure energy. There are no polarities or identities in the "being" world because they are not necessary or needed.

Who do you think you are? Your body? Your thoughts? Your feelings? Your accomplishments? Your mind? You are not the person in your mind; you are the energy observing the person in your mind. Some of you may not grasp this concept right away. That is fine for now, this is just a brief overview and not a detailed description. You do not need to comprehend this for your healing. As you move further along, this will come to you – at your pace.

What I am trying to establish is, we are not the labels others or ourselves place on us. This journey will serve to help you disassociate yourself from your labels and to heighten your awareness. To discover you are much more than a label.

The biggest obstacle you may face is your identity with your feelings, emotions, addictions and state of health. "I am needy", "I am shy", "I am a loser", "I have medical issues", or "I am a gambler". If these labels have been marked on you for years, the terror of releasing them can be overwhelming. "This is how I have known myself to be for as long as I can remember. Who will I be if not the identity I currently am? This is the only way I know myself."

Yes, it can be frightful to become someone you don't have a clue about even when it is for the better. That is why you need to do this work at your own pace, the changes will happen for you naturally. Will fear stand in the way? Probably. Fear is a constant that needs to be dealt with head on during your healing journey. Fear is not to be feared but to be faced. For some it will be easier for others, but as I have discussed prior, do not let fear stop you from becoming the person you deserve to be.

Jealousy, Bitterness, Resentment

The jealous person treats their partner as a possession instead of a unique individual. The jealous person in intimate relationships can stem from being overly needy, attention-starved, being insecure and other false needs. Jealousy is not a sign of love; it is a sign of something amiss. Chances are, within the jealous person are deep-seated insecurities.

I'm not talking about the feelings of jealousy that may be felt within a healthy relationship and understood on a mature level; I am talking about the extreme form of jealousy. When a jealous person is enraged due to any perceived threat from someone invading their space, including their possessions, there are no boundaries on the part of the jealous person. And without having boundaries than any misfortune can happen – "acts of passion" they are called when crime is involved. It should be called "when the insecurity monster is unleashed from within".

When you feel jealousy due to someone else's good, it is a symptom of how unhappy you are with yourself and your life. People who are happy and content with their life are rarely jealous. There is no need since they are content. There are people whose life is not full of contentment, yet still be happy for others. There is no need within them to be jealous.

Look at jealousy as a symptom. It is covering up something deeper than jealousy. Are you miserable for the choices you have made in life? Do you wish you looked different, acted different, and could be like him or her? Do you think how that person is moving forward and there you are stuck, you cannot move, you think you need to stay? What makes you think you are so stuck? Fear is the reason, the rest are excuses.

Bitterness and resentment will eat away at you. Diseases spring forth from bitterness and resentment. These are hard-felt obstacles to carry with you; they do damage. To be mad at the world, to resent your life, your choices, to be forever bitter at the one who hurt you; it is so easy to get caught in this web. So you say to yourself, "Ok, I will stop being bitter and resentful. It's true, I don't want it anymore" and so you bury it. But burying it does not release it; it only forces it deeper within your body which causes more stress.

By finding the source of your bitterness and resentment, you are then able to recognize it, and replace it with healthy thought patterns. Is there not a bit of curiosity about what it would be like to live without these burdens plaguing your mind endlessly, day in and day out?

Resistance

As you travel along on your path of discovery and healing, you will have as companions, fear and resistance. At the start, realize that it does no good in trying to make them go away, they won't. The more you fight them, the more control they will have. If you know fear and resistance are part of the package plan, then you can have an easier time of accepting them and allowing them to be. As you travel deeper on your path, resistance and fear begin to fade and lose their strength. Resistance and fear is what holds us back from succeeding, from venturing into new territory, and from doing what is right and good for us.

Resistance comes disguised in many forms, cleaning the house instead of working on ourselves, going shopping instead of facing situations in your life, ignoring problems hoping they go away on their own, being moody, angry, the list goes on and on. Procrastination, laziness, and fatigue are also signs of resistance. Having attitudes of "I know it all" and "I don't need this" are ways of stopping you. I resisted acknowledging that I suffered traumatic experiences as a child, that my way of living wasn't working, and that I needed to work on myself in order to heal my life. Instead of resisting resistance, I have come to accept it as an integral part of healing. It shows us where we are stuck. It shows us what we do not want to face about ourselves or others.

We expend an enormous amount of energy repressing emotions. So the choice becomes, "Do I keep repressing or do I let it up and out in order to be free?" And we wonder why our lives do not work. Look at the heavy burdens we are carrying within. When we take our power back from resistance and fear, we start to see clearly how attached we are to our misery, our fears, and our problems.

Resistance can interject when we are on the verge of a breakthrough or a positive change happening. For some of us, just before the event occurs, we get a rush of resistance and fear. Deeply rooted, we feel that we do not deserve good in our lives. So, we sabotage the good and do not receive it, or we allow it in despite our nervousness.

One form of resistance is when we know we should be doing "A" but do "B" instead. And we do this day in and day out. We need to ask ourselves, "Why do I keep avoiding 'A'?" As usual fear and resistance are keeping you from tackling "A", but why? Do you think and/or feel that "A" is too emotional to deal with, too confrontational, or too intense? These are all resistance mechanisms. Are you being lazy about it, procrastinating, do not know where to begin, or too comfy in your present misery to move forward? Again, resistance. Do you need professional assistance, but do not want to reach out?

This is not something to beat yourself up about or feel guilt or shame. What you are doing is educating yourself as to your behavior without judgment or criticism or condemnation. When you realize and recognize that you are not doing "A" that in itself is a huge step toward clearing away what is obstructing your progress. Did you even realize that last year you were avoiding "A"? Probably not, but now you do. Consciously say to yourself, "I am avoiding 'A'. I see that now." Feel proud that you can see it and for bringing it up and out instead of sweeping it under the rug yet again. So now you know you are avoiding "A" which is great, but it still begs the question, why? You need to ask yourself that question and write down your answer(s). See *The "Why" Question Process* under the *Helpful Tools* section.

Here is an example:

- "Why am I avoiding 'A'?"
  Facing what I am avoiding requires a change in my life and my way of thinking. I know it is a beneficial change. But even though I know it is beneficial for me, it is also overwhelming for me.

- "Why is it so overwhelming?"
  I do not know where to begin.

- "Why not?"
  This is all new to me.

- "Why don't I seek some form of assistance?"
  Than that means I actually have to *do* something. No, I don't want to. Leave me alone, I like where I am…safe and miserable and that's how I like it, so there! Now just go away!

- "Why don't I think and/or feel I deserve something better?"
  Me? Have a better life emotionally, physically, spiritually, intellectually, materially? No, no, no. I am so use to the misery I know. It's safe and secure and miserable. Me, do something positive for myself? That's a first.

- "Why not?"
  Because way down deep inside I feel I don't deserve it.

- "Now we are getting somewhere. Why don't I deserve a happy, healthy, prosperous, loving life?"
  Because my parents, guardians, siblings, teachers, friends, whoever constantly put me down, criticized me, mocked me, and made me feel inferior, like I am worthless.

- "Why did this person(s) put me down or criticize me, etc.?"
  Because they don't know any better? Because they are hiding their own insecurities? Because that's how they were raised?

- "So then why am I allowing these people's thoughts, opinions, and beliefs to control and influence my life today?"
  Because I didn't look at it like this before. I did not know that what happened to me during my growing years affects the way I think, feel, and behave today.

- "But it does, very much so. So am I willing to start changing these patterns inside me?"
  I am willing. I am terrified but I still want to. I do not want people's ignorance dictating my life anymore. I want the life I deserve. I want to fix what is broke inside. The person(s) of my initial misery is not what is important now. What is important is facing who I am and fixing me.

There is no blame, there is only fixing. This is all
about learning how to love me the way I deserve
too; this does not mean in a selfish way.

As you write down your answers and ask yourself why to your
previous answer you go deeper and deeper down until what is
repressed and hidden starts to shake loose and emerge.

There are different levels we all have. There is the surface
level, "Well that's the way I am, I was born this way." Most people
stop at this level and go no further; resigning themselves that there
is nothing that can be done about their life and their problems.
There are much deeper levels under that, like the layers of an
onion, until you hit the core which is the true essence of why you
are the way you are.

Sometimes I would clean an already clean house and realize
that I was doing this so I did not have to process painful emotions,
memories, thoughts, etc. I did not want to see the "not so great
aspects" of myself. I would stop and say, "I know I am resisting, I
do not have the energy, interest, or desire to feel what I must. I'm
too tired, I can't do it and I do not want to! Just leave me alone
and GO AWAY!" But as tired as I was, and as drained as I was, I
knew what I needed to do in order to heal.

Your desire to be the person you deserve to be, to discover the
pure being that you are, to meet yourself for the first time, must
be ever present in your mind. Your desire, determination, and
persistence will keep resistance away. My desire to vanquish all
the wrong beliefs, attitudes, and feelings that were instilled in me
was greater than any form of resistance thrown at me.

Do not forget that you deserve to have healthy beliefs,
attitudes and feelings about yourself. That you deserve to live a
life of health, wealth and joy. It is okay to rid yourself of unhealthy
and false beliefs instilled in you during your growing years. Was

I perfect about overcoming resistance each and every time? Of course not. Did I beat myself up over it? No. Did I have to nudge myself at times, even a kick in the pants to get going, yes I did.

There is a difference between taking a break and resisting. And yes it is a fine line between the two, but that is where the body comes in and not the mind. The body knows when you are resisting versus when you need a break. Ask the body, feel the body...it will tell you.

What gives resistance its edge? Fear. No fear; no resistance. Remember, you deserve to overcome these false obstacles and barriers. Do not let resistance stop the process.

Self-doubt, Self-hatred, No Self-Confidence, No Self-Esteem

You may read the title of this topic and think, "What a mess! Isn't there anything about me I like or is good?" You have plenty of good though you may not allow yourself to see it. Every day write three things that you do well or good things about you, even if you need to start with something like, "I have nice eyebrows." There are tons of stuff we do well every day and we have inner and outer treasures to be grateful for.

So we have issues; that doesn't make us bad people. We are, on the whole, good people that perhaps could use some overhauling and updating…a newer model so to speak! Be aware of your good qualities, be thankful for what you do have, don't gripe over what you do not have. If all you do is moan and complain then you allow no room for growth. As long as you keep feeling sorry for yourself, then you don't have to take a real look at your life.

As you gain in understanding of yourself, when you start getting answers to why you behave and act the way you do, your self-image changes also. As you become aware of who you are, you will notice, ever so slightly, that you do not think of yourself the way you use to. Your self-confidence rises naturally in direct proportion to the insights you gain about yourself. So, as your self-confidence increases naturally, your feelings of self-lack decreases. As one rises, the other falls.

Self-doubt decreases as your self-confidence rises. You feel better about yourself. So for now, put your self-negatives to the side and concentrate instead on the how's and why's you have developed those self-negatives. If you decide to complain about how you have no self-confidence, that you are such an idiot, and how much you hate yourself, that is a clear indication of resistance from getting to know yourself better. If you would rather wallow in your pity party, then so be it, that is your decision. I know how comfortable it is there; miserable, oh yes it is, but oh so cozy too. It is much easier to whine your life away instead of actually taking action.

And who would you be if you didn't condemn yourself anymore – you would be lost without that identity. When you decide to dig in your heels, take a deep breathe, and say "Okay, I will do the work, it may be hard at times, but I want to do it anyway." The most amazing thing happens over time; how grateful you are to yourself that you did go ahead and walk the healing path. How you fought the fear and the resistance and faced the feelings and the pain only to come out the other side renewed with a truer sense of self that you ever thought possible. Yes, it will be rough at times, but it sure won't be boring. Every day I am grateful for having the courage to do it because when I look back, I cannot believe that person was actually me.

You have to cross the swamp to get to the other shore and the smile on your face will be genuine since it comes from the deepest reaches of your psyche. You made it. You did it!

SELF-PUNISHMENT/ SELF-DESTRUCTION/ SELF-SABOTAGE

Some of us have a strong need for suffering, torment, and punishment. A lot of us do it unconsciously. We have a need to fail or we come just within reach of our goal, but do not attain it. We may be financially successful but suffer horribly in our personal life.

Most of us aren't even aware we are doing this to ourselves. We are conditioned from an early age to believe things about ourselves that are negative and not true. But if this belief and behavior is all we have known, than for us it is normal. Some of us don't even recognize it as misery or self-hatred since it has been with us since our growing years. It is a part of us, it is who we are. But on closer inspection, is it really who we are? Of course not. We were molded a certain way, and we are capable of remolding ourselves.

Self-destruction doesn't have to be in a grand form; little acts against ourselves are just as telling. Our need to sabotage ourselves stays alive by consistently making unhealthy decisions, and engaging in unhealthy actions. For many of us self-destruction is a core belief, it is our foundation.

Do not mistake financial success or a successful marriage or being a grade "A" student as not having these tendencies also. You may be a grade "A" student but you think you are the ugliest person in the school. So you destroy your body by overeating, undereating, cutting, random sex, etc. The need to self-punish can come from a number of sources - actual punishment, criticisms, insults, beatings, abuse are all but a few examples. We continue the punishment as adults since we believe we need to be punished.

Self-punishment is a symptom and can be a form of coping as are the other obstacles and barriers in our lives. The good news is that we can remold, reshape and reprogram our brains; we can create new chemical and electrical impulses and pathways.

I wish I had a magic wand and just wave it over the world, and have everything and everyone on it healed, healthy, happy and prosperous. But no, it must be done the old-fashioned way, one step at a time; because that's the way it works. If you think you are going to rush through this process, think again. Why rush anyway? Don't you want to do it the right way the first time around? Or do you want to keep punishing yourself and blindly rushing through it - only to have to face it all over again. As a gift to yourself, isn't it time to lay down the gauntlet and pick up a peace symbol instead?

Suffering/Worrying

It is amazing when we get further along and look back, and see how much our suffering affected the way we lived, how worry took from us precious time. This internal suffering started during our growing years and we continue on with it as adults. We find ourselves: working in a negative environment, maintaining unhealthy relationships, and engaging in addictions and obsessions to name a few.

You might hate your job, but it's a steady paycheck. You may despise your spouse, but you are not living alone. The thought of changing what is comfortable and secure is terrifying. You may be miserable but it's familiar, and we like familiar.

I'm not saying that everyone should quit their jobs and get divorced, I am only pointing out that our internal suffering and worrying can cause us to stay stuck. Instead of shutting out or ignoring your pain, admit to yourself it is there and it does exist, but it doesn't have to stay that way. We do have options. We are in a self-made prison but there are no locks for there is no cell; it is an illusion we use to keep us stuck where we are.

Our suffering is calling out to us – it wants us to heal. It is trying to tell us something. Did you ever ask yourself, "Why do I allow myself to suffer?" If you answer "I have no choice" then perhaps you do not know the way out, or you prefer to suffer. You can continue to live with the unproductive toxic pain (the pain you live with every day) or you can live with productive pain. Productive pain is the pain that moves you forward to healing and wholeness. Productive pain is temporary unlike your daily toxic pain which stays with you.

I am not saying that life won't have its challenges or issues to deal with, but you will handle them differently, with acquired clarity from unlearning. There will be issues that stick to you like glue and that you will need to visit and revisit. The healing path is truly about the journey for it is during the journey when the insights and changes occur.

And to the worriers in the group – we both know that worrying gets us nowhere, but it gives us plenty of wasted time. Worry stems from having our mind in the past or in the future. When we stay present, worry does not have a place to hang its hat.

Your Own Mind/Your Ego

Of course, we need our brains for our day to day existence. Decisions need to be made, choices decided, and quick reactions are necessary to immediate life situations. On your healing path, the mind and ego will insert thoughts of doubt, fear, illusions, incorrect answers and anything else to keep you from advancing. The mind is great for daily living, but not for your healing work.

It is the body and your being side who knows what is right or not. If you have the attitude of knowing it all, it blocks answers from coming. Of course we need our brains for this journey, but some people seem to think they cannot change what they think. Why? You are the one thinking it; you are the one allowing it in your brain. You and only you control what you choose to think and believe.

Does it take persistence in order to change long held thought patterns and ways of thinking…yes it does. Can it be challenging at times, oh yes it can. Look past what needs to be done and focus on the end result which is a new and improved you!

Years ago, when I first started replacing negative thoughts with positive ones, I could only do it on a small scale and little by little. I would repeat in my head, "I want to change, I want to change." I would tell myself over and over, "I am safe. It is safe for me to love and be loved. I love me. I love all of me." Did I believe what I was saying at first? No. Did persistence and determination help in changing my ways of thinking? Yes. Even my first attempts at living in the present hurt my brain, so to speak. I was so ingrained with living in either the past or the future or obsessing about some hurtful situation; living in the present was like learning a foreign language.

Anything we begin anew has a learning curve. Do you think pianists just sit down and start playing or that a star athlete became that way overnight? Little league and piano teachers exist for a reason. As does practice, practice, practice.

As we allow ourselves to open up, to hold the belief that everything is going to be okay, we are in a position to receive answers that seem to come from outside ourselves but actually come from within. The answers will either pop into your psyche like it came from nowhere, or you may hear the answer on the radio, television, or someone speaking. It may come from reading or a dream. It isn't the same as you thinking and thinking and coming up with answers. I have found, for the healing work, the answers just come naturally. Not from your ego, not from your brain, but deep inside where your energy extends farther out beyond your human form. There is a difference when you insert the answer intellectually, from when you allow the answer to come naturally.

SECTION 4

HELPFUL TOOLS
(TO HELP US DIG)

AFFIRMATIONS

Some people say affirmations work incredibly well and others say they do not work at all. Either view is valid, they work or they don't. So how can we create affirmations that work for us? It depends on various factors. How the affirmation is used, the words that are chosen, the surface feeling behind the affirmation as well as the deep-rooted belief, and the internal state of the person are some of the factors to take into account. When working with affirmations we need to be flexible and experimental. The statements need to be read slowly and with as much emotion as you can muster. Saying an affirmation with no thought, meaning, or emotion behind it will do you no good.

Affirming all day that, "I am wealthy" will not get you very far if deep down you possess a "poverty is me" belief. It may be better to just declare "Wealth". Affirmations are used alongside the unlearning of yourself. As you work on an issue, let's say gambling for instance, you go deep within and find the reason or the source of why you gamble. As you unravel your need to gamble, you are, at the same time, using affirmations to help loosen the unconscious grip the false belief has on you.

Then there are those who say that polarity is involved: if you are saying, "I am wealthy" than your mind concludes that actually you are poor. So than by saying, "I am poor" concludes that actually I am wealthy? Polarities, opposites, are around us at all times. For me, I have found this concept does not hinder my progress using affirmations; it is more of the words used and the feelings felt that affects the desired outcome. The statement has to feel good within you; if it doesn't, it will not work (see *Words* in the *Grounding Information* section). Affirmations are used to improve yourself, to aid in transforming unhealthy patterns into healthy ones. False and unhealthy beliefs, attitudes, perceptions, thinking, and feeling are intertwined and need to be undone and replaced with healthier viewpoints. Affirmations are a great tool to use during the process.

You may use affirmations to help another heal, to send the person love and light, and to affirm for another's well-being. They are not used to try to get another whether in love or revenge. For me, affirmations played and still play a significant role in my healing process. Affirmations can be vital in helping to create healthy new brain pathways. Repeating an affirmation at least five times spread throughout the day can benefit you. Affirm upon arising, mid-morning, afternoon, evening, and before retiring for bed with the two most crucial being upon arising and before going to sleep. The others can be said as you see fit.

The time frame for each individual is unique. Your body will know what to do. If you feel you need to keep repeating it, than repeat it. I have repeated statements over and over throughout the course of the day when necessary. I may say an affirmation 100 times, or a 1000 times if I feel the need to. Sometimes I use affirmations to replace a negative thought that slips into my brain, and so I need to repeat and repeat until the negativity dissipates. I prefer putting my energy into a positive statement versus the strain of obsessing on a negative thought.

People call affirmations requests. Affirmations are statements that are true, they are not hopeful desires. Your brain may wholeheartedly believe an affirmation to be true, but your heart is like "No way, I do not believe a word of it." That is because the information from the brain has not yet filtered into the heart and into the subconscious. Just keep going. Believing the statement to be true in the brain is half the aim. And if you can make it halfway, than you certainly can make it all the way! Which feels stronger for you: "a request" or "a true and powerful statement"? What mindset do you think will work best - believing they are requests, hopes, and wishes, or knowing that affirmations are true and powerful statements?

Affirmations when written, spoken, or read need to stir something within you. That is how you know they are working. You feel a good feeling within or a stirring of some kind. You feel a change within. Well you may ask, "How can I feel it in my heart when it's not there yet? It's in my head, but not my heart." If you believe it in your head that means it is working, and if you keep undoing and unlearning it will reach your heart. If you do not believe it in your head, you need to start by saying, "I am willing to change." If resistance is blocking your progress, repeat over and over, "I am willing to change." Little by little all that gunk that is compacted within you will start to shift and loosen.

I felt unlovable for many years. When I started affirming, "I am lovable" and other related affirmations, I knew it in my head but felt nothing in my heart. I said my affirmations anyway and I did use my heart when I said them knowing this belief would soak into the deepest reaches of my mind and body. It took time and a lot of unlearning along with the affirmations, but now in my heart of hearts, I know, feel, and believe I am very lovable. I was uncovering the source of my false belief and at the same time saying related affirmations.

There are times when I get an inner signal to stop affirming. If the signal comes from my mind, the chances are I am resisting the work or perhaps I need a break. Ask your body, and not your brain, "Am I resisting?" If you feel a dreadful tug inside, anywhere in the body, it very well could be resistance. If you don't feel that, then ask the body, "Do I need to stop a while, do I need a break?" If your body shouts "Yes!" then listen to your body and take a break. If the body signal is clear to stop affirming then do so. Allow time for the brain and body to do its work; for the feeling to flow down into the heart and take hold. It's like exercising a muscle; you need to work it, than rest it, in order to get stronger and healthier.

I cannot give you exact time frames; this work involves learning to listen to the body which is covered in the next guidebook. There is no time on your healing path; this work does not include clock time. Some issues I overcame with ease and within one day. Others took days, and others weeks and even months. The most deep-rooted issues will take the longest, but time isn't the goal. The goal is to become the person you deserve to be; to wipe out for good the nasty habits that keep you embroiled in your daily misery.

"I have to be saying this stuff for the rest of my life?" Would you rather worry about the future, regret the past, or obsess how this one or that one treated you, or would you rather start your day affirming good things happening for you today?

Let's go through an affirmation exercise (Use whatever scenario fits you, I used smoking for the example):

> You quit smoking and over time you notice that you lost some of your bravery. Now that you no longer smoke, there is this slight apprehension you haven't felt before.

> You realize that you used smoking as a smoke screen to keep people at a distance. It was your shield; your protective armor, which gave you

courage. Now you feel raw and naked without your smoke shield; you feel exposed.

You then connect to how shy you were as a child; how you hid behind your mother. Shyness is fear. Why were you so afraid of people? For this example, you were told that people were bad, very bad and that people would hurt you if you let them in. So you developed a belief that people are out to hurt you, but as an adult you need to interact with society so cigarettes were a great shield for you. You could interact with people, but the smoke kept a veil between you and them.

As an adult, you really don't trust people. It's not that you don't have relationships or that you don't hug people, but there was always this "backed-off" necessity inside you that you took as normal all your life. But now you can see where it has caused you some unfortunate occurrences in your life, and so you want to be rid of this false belief and create a new healthy belief. Plus you probably had many people in your life that did hurt you since your belief was that people hurt you. Since you have an unconscious need to keep this belief alive, you attract those that reinforce the belief "people hurt me".

Taking pen and paper, write down your answers to, "What do I want to change?"

-   The belief that people are out to get me.
-   To know, believe, and feel that people care about me.

- I don't need an artificial shield to protect me.
- I have all the courage I need on my own.
- I no longer need to fear people. I have solid judgment skills and immediately recognize the early warning signs of an unhealthy situation.

"How do I know which of these five are the most important for me to concentrate on?" Read each one out loud, and notice how the body reacts. Somewhere in your body, your chest, your hand, your stomach, your gut, ear, leg, wherever, there will be a reaction. And for those who cannot feel right now, how does your brain react when you say it? What do you think about the statement? Don't overthink it; go with your first impression.

You have listed five changes you want to incorporate into your life. Your list may have many more, or less. Speak your listed changes out loud, the body will react whereas if you say them silently, the body may not react at all. Decide which one has the strongest response. If there is one in particular that stands out, then that is the one to start with. Or, you may want to work on the stronger one last and work on the weaker ones first. At times when I worked on the stronger ones first, the weaker-felt ones changed automatically as I did the stronger ones first.

Work on one at a time. Feel which ones causes a reaction in the body. Let's say all 5 do. We need to distinguish which ones we want to do first, and for some of you, you will automatically know which one you want. For others, the body will react and cry out, "That one, do that one." Let's say you feel nothing for all five, which at this point could be an indication of resistance. Choose the one that stands out for you in some way, or pick one you think is most important.

For this example, I chose "To know, believe, and feel that people care about me." Remember that currently you firmly believe that people do not care about you so saying an affirmation such as, "Everyone cares about me" will not resonate within and therefore not be absorbed. Affirmations are best when concise and to the point. One or two concise statements works well. In the beginning though, it sometimes is necessary to unhinge and loosen the old belief so it surfaces. As the old belief is loosened, then updated affirmations will be used, and there will be less of them.

> "I no longer need to believe that no one cares about me and therefore no longer need to attract these types of people into my life. This was instilled in me from unhealthy sources and it is untrue and so I release this belief for good. I no longer need or want it. There are people who care about me and I care about them and I am willing to attract them to me more and more every day."

Some people add a closing affirmation such as:

All is well.
I am safe.
I love me.
I am loved.
I love.
I now change.
I want to change.
Thank you.
I deserve the best.
I am free.

Over time you notice the impact of the affirmations are losing their strength and meaning. It could mean you need to take a break from saying them or the words are not resonating within. You may need to rephrase the statement. It can also mean you have moved up the ladder of awareness and the meaning has taken hold. Let's say you now know in your head and heart that there are people out there who care for you. You no longer have doubts. You fully realize it and believe it. You can then alter your affirmation to read something like:

> "The people who now enter my life care about me
> as I care about them."

Perhaps you will need to say this for reinforcement or to further instill it in your belief system or the best outcome – you no longer need it! You get it, you got it, and you have changed in this area.

When I first read out loud, "I am safe", my stomach twisted in knots from unease and fear. I was surprised for when I read it silently, I did not receive the same response. When I read it out loud, I felt my body react. That is when I realized, consciously, for the first time, that I did not feel safe. I didn't feel safe at all. And so the unlearning, undoing, and creating began.

You may need to go back over older affirmations; there's nothing wrong with a refresher, it's a good idea to keep your affirmations for future use. When I read older affirmations, it shows the progress of my journey. It amazes me to read old statements and see what I once believed. It can be mind-blowing – in a good way of course. It is a great feeling to look back and see how far you have come.

Is it sad that you have to fix and change so much? Yes it is. You can acknowledge that, but spin around quick and start walking forward again, no need to wallow over what could have been. Instead, be proud of yourself for progressing and be thankful for how you have learned and are learning still. Once you feel a sense of accomplishment, no matter how small, your momentum to enact change gathers speed. The desire for change becomes stronger than the desire to wallow. Do not forget your bedfellows of fear and resistance; they will be with you every step of the way trying to hinder or stop your progress. You will reach a certain point where you stare down and stand up to your interferences. Your accomplishments push you to do good for yourself. This is when fear and resistance start to lose their firm grip on you.

You are saying your affirmations and you expect your mess to disappear and for it to happen quickly. At times, it does work fast, other times not so fast. Affirmations help loosen stuck patterns we hold deep inside. These statements of truth help bring these issues to the surface.

Use words that work for you; that stir a warm feeling or thought somewhere in your body. For those who cannot feel at the moment, then use your brain for what "thinks" right for you instead of what "feels" right for you.

AFFIRMATION NOTES

1. Determine what area/issue/condition/symptom you want to work on.
2. What do you want to change in this area? List all the changes you desire. Your body will say, "Yes, that is the one I want to start with." Sometimes accomplishing one change will have a domino effect and the other desires of change will change automatically.
3. By reading aloud, which one(s) resonated strongly for you inside your body?
4. Pick the ones that speak to you the loudest. Try to stay with 1 or 2 at the same time.
5. Create your own affirmation or you can use my affirmation supplement or search the web or any material you have in your home or the library, etc. Use affirmations you believe in; use ones that resonate within you.

AFFIRMATIONS DO'S AND DON'TS.

In no way does this list contain all the available forms of affirmations that exist. I compiled an "I" use and don't use list to help you get started. There are numerous variations (see the Affirmation supplement with this guidebook series).

USE	DO NOT USE
I am	I will (will is future in this case; the future doesn't ever arrive!)
I have (I now have)	I will be
I do	I wish (future)
I am willing	I hope (future)
I no longer need	
I now	
I accept (I now accept)	
I receive (I now receive)	
I know and feel (I now know and feel)	
I allow (I now allow)	
I am aware (I am now aware)	
I view	
I see	
I know	

Let's look at ways of expressing affirmations:

"I will get better."

(No, you probably won't or if you do, it may take a very long time. "I will" refers to the future and the future never arrives. Your statements need to be in the present, like right now.)

"I am getting better and better every day."

(Still a future event by using "getting". It can be used as a start point to get you up and going, but after that dropping the "getting" will have you back in the present where you want to be)

"I am better and better every day."

(This is in the present.)

Or if you are stuck:

"I am willing to get better and better every day because I want to and I deserve to."

(You're willing to "get" it, which is something you are after. When your confidence grows and you start believing, drop the "willing to get".

Or

"I no longer need to believe that I will not get better. I get better and better every day."

Can you see the difference between:

I will
I get
I wish
I hope
and
I have
I am
I do

The first four are future while the last three are present; you already **have** it, you're not **getting** it.

The shorter and more concise the affirmation is, the better. One or two lines work well. At times you may need to extend the affirmation, which is fine, especially when you are removing a tough block or inner obstacle during the early stages of working on a false belief. Remember do what feels good for you. Be flexible; sometimes a short sentence is enough; at other times a few statements may be needed. One word is a great way to allow new situations to enter your life. Saying one word speaks volumes when said with feeling or meaning. Say it with meaning, believe what you are stating.

Let's look at how Joseph Murphy in *The Power of Your Subconscious Mind* describes how affirming for wealth fails and his remedy for it:

I have talked to many people during the past thirty-five years whose usual complaint is, "I have said for weeks and months, 'I am wealthy, I am prosperous', and nothing has happened." I discovered that when they said, "I am prosperous,

I am wealthy," they felt within that they were lying to themselves. One man told me, "I have affirmed that I am prosperous until I am tired. Things are now worse. I knew when I made the statement that it was obviously not true." His statements were rejected by the conscious mind, and the very opposite of what he outwardly affirmed and claimed was made manifest.

Your affirmation succeeds best when it is specific and when it does not produce a mental conflict or argument; hence the statements made by this man made matters worse because they suggested his lack. Your subconscious accepts what you really feel to be true, not just idle words or statements. The dominant idea or belief is always accepted by the subconscious mind.

The following is an excellent way to overcome this conflict for those who have this difficulty. Make this practical statement frequently, particularly prior to sleep: "By day and by night I am being prospered in all of my interests." This affirmation will not arouse any argument because it does not contradict your subconscious mind's impression of financial lack.

When I affirmed, "I am safe" I didn't feel safe inside. For me, it wasn't a true statement though the statement itself is true. Since my reaction to this statement was so strong, I kept on saying it in order to loosen up fixed ideas in my head plus I wanted to know why I didn't feel safe. So even though I felt the statement to be untrue for me, I still had an inner need to express it.

According to Joseph Murphy, I needed to state something that didn't cause argument inside and that is where, "I am willing..." comes into play. "I am willing to feel safe." In my case stating "I feel safe" didn't change me into feeling safe, what it did do was loosen up and bring to the surface the issues why I didn't feel safe. That's why flexibility is necessary with affirmations. Sometimes you have this inner knowing to keep on saying what you are affirming; other times the affirmation will do nothing for you and needs to be rewritten or revised.

If you absolutely do not believe what you are saying than start out using, "I am willing". "I am willing to love myself. I am willing to change. I am willing to start thinking in healthier ways." As you heal, you will be able to drop the "I am willing". "I love myself. I change. I think healthy ways." A big hug of thanks to Louise Hay author of *You Can Heal Your Life* for teaching me about "I am willing". It has been a gift for me over and over again.

When used properly, affirmations work, and work well all throughout your healing process. Transformation work needs to be offset by down time and fun time. This is not all work and no play - my goodness what fun would that not be!

PITY PARTY

- Victim mentality.
- Woe is me.
- Feel sorry for me.
- It's all their fault.
- I'm the innocent victim here.
- You change so I feel better.
- You do the work, I'm too messed up.
- It's all about me.
- Take care of me so I don't have to.
- Blaming the other.

And there are those:

- It's all my fault.
- Nothing good happens to me
- Why can't I be like him/her?
- How come everything good happens to them?
- I have no luck.
- No one takes care of me.
- If you were raised like me, then you would understand.

The joys of self-pity: the whining, the wallowing, the moaning, the complaining. "Save me, just save me, it's up to you to do it, not me." For some, this is a familiar scenario whether it is yourself or someone you know. They just want to complain and do nothing or almost nothing to help themselves. They want the world to feel sorry for them. They can come across as being powerless or having an air of entitlement; that the world owes them.

When they do get what they are whining about they find fault with it. This type of mentality, self-pity, is a bottomless pit inside the person that cannot ever be satisfied. As much as you do for them, it still is not enough. When they can no longer gripe about the current want, they move on to their next complaint and unfulfilled desire. These people always have unfulfilled desires; there is no satisfying this mind set. When you give them what they want, it isn't good enough, they want more. These people cannot be pleased any way you try.

Some of us spend our lives trying to make someone else happy and this person who, in their current state, is incapable of feeling happiness. They absolutely connect with their misery on a grand scale. These people have any excuse in the book as to why they cannot do something or why it isn't their fault. To me, it seems like the "woe is me" attitude comes from a child's standpoint and not an adults. Another pity method is the classic narcissist and/or control freak that uses pity as a manipulation tool and as a means to get themselves out of problems or troubles.

Maybe the only way people could get attention from their caregivers was to create some kind of drama in order for the caretaker to take notice and fix whatever problem the child conjured up. Maybe these people were ignored as children and are starving for attention. Maybe the parents or caretakers did anything and everything for them and now cannot fend for themselves. They revert into child-like mode in order to get things done for them.

Perhaps they were not taught specific skills and are reluctant to do things on their own; they dread appearing stupid. And then there are those who were yelled at and criticized for trying to accomplish something on their own. Their ability to achieve success were undermined by constant insults and criticism. Now, as an adult, they are terrified of failure or even trying to achieve something on their own. There are those, when they did fail, were met with mocking, insults, and taunting to the point where failure is synonymous with humiliation and heightened levels of shame. Or the little pouting boy or girl not getting their way, feel sorry for me mommy and/or daddy and the parents give in to their child's every whim.

The fear of humiliation, shame, guilt, or rejection may be so intense for these people that it literally stops them from living a life of satisfaction and contentment. Aren't you the least bit curious as to why you live in a world of self-pity and/or blaming others? Though you were conditioned this way doesn't mean you have to stay this way.

If you are the one trying to appease these people; you need to stop and ask yourself why. Perhaps you were trained early on to care for others without your needs being met. You developed certain co-dependent tendencies that others came first before you. Perhaps you put others first and their problems so you don't have to deal with your own. Maybe you hate yourself so much, you believe your life isn't worth anything. By attending to another's needs it allows you to stick your head in the sand and ignore what is going on in your life. By attending to another's need on a constant basis, you do not have to feel what is inside you. By attending to another, you do not have to confront your own pain. You are too busy nurturing the other's pain and misery. I am sure there are more I have not listed. Regardless of how you were raised or what was said, your life deserves to be lived and expressed with joy and contentment. There is no obligation to have heaviness within.

"Why, pray tell, are you writing about self-pity people in the *Helpful Tools* section of the guidebook?" To illustrate the difference between a fixed mind set, and a temporary self-imposed pity party. There are times, as we go through phases of our healing, that we need to acknowledge certain situations of our lives. We need to feel the sorrow that arises from these situations. I have found that by acknowledging, and not denying or ignoring our sorrow, it tends to release itself from us. Of course we are going to feel anger and sorrow for the way we were treated, that cannot be denied or buried. It needs to come up and out so it can be gone for good.

You have every right to feel anguish, anger, rage, sorrow, self-pity as you awaken to aspects of your life that you kept hidden deep within. It is all part of the restorative process. I worked on my healing and realized certain dynamics of my upbringing. After it soaked in, I went through the grieving process and part of that process included rage and feeling sorry for myself. I felt sorry for me because someone else that was mentally inept caused me hurt and pain.

I allowed myself to feel complete sorrow and grief for not receiving the proper love, care and nurturing I required during my growing years. I was worth something. So I plopped on the couch, zoned out in front of the television, feeling sorry for myself and mad at the world, emotionally eating all along the way. After the sorrow came the rage. Everyone was so much better off than me. I had nothing, was nothing, and no one cared. I had intense rage because I had to fix me and it wasn't even my fault.

This crap was instilled in me by ignorant, selfish people and now I had to clean up their mess. Talk about unfair. They get away with horrendous acts of misconduct and here I am, the garbage sweeper, dealing with and fixing the crap they left behind. I let myself collapse into my self-pity, frustration, sorrow, and rage.

I went to bed that night feeling empty. The next day I awoke and I amazingly felt stronger; like something had lifted off my shoulders. I felt empowered. My thinking was clearer, I felt lighter. I was back on track and happy about it. My determination and desire to fix me was as strong as ever. The people who hurt me were no longer an obstacle, they were out of my way. I wanted to fix me. I wanted to live a life that I chose and not one forced on me by outside influences. I thanked God for listening to me vent. I can tell God anything and everything and He still loves me unconditionally. He knows me better than everyone, He loves me more than anyone, and He understands the deep hidden workings of me. I read a church sign that said, "Pray anywhere for God is everywhere."

I was grateful the self-pity was gone, it is such a heavy energy. I had a nice relaxing me day. I did things I enjoyed; I treated myself to treats and gifts, just little things, nothing major and not all of them cost money. I love walking in nature and have some favorite spots. I was grateful I was back on track. I appreciated that I needed to release and vent all the inner grief, sorrow and rage I held inside for so long. That a day or two of pity partying was actually good for the mind and body as it helped release toxicity. Keep in mind, this is a temporary state of self-pity as are the other intense emotions we are releasing.

I found it necessary to have these intermittent pity parties when the body needed it in order to progress my healing. I equated it with a fireplace needing a chimney for the smoke to billow up and out of the house safely. Or the plumbing vents that rise above our roofs to allow the gasses to escape from the plumbing system. Without chimneys and without vents where would the smoke and gasses end up; trapped inside the house. So perhaps we humans need to vent our inner damages in order for us to maintain a sturdy house within. The good news is, the more we release, the less need to vent.

Did you notice I did not engage anyone in the pity party but me? I did not call and whine and moan to friends and family. I kept it between me and my Creator. I did not call and scream at the people who hurt me. I didn't make it a neighborhood "feel sorry for me gala". It was only for me in order to cope with releasing deep inner emotion, and not to seek pity from others. If you need to share it with a support group, professional, trusted companion, or friend then do so if that will help you heal. If you are doing it looking for attention, then know that is the reason why you are reaching out. No judging, no condemning, just being aware of who you are.

If speaking with a Higher Power or another person doesn't do it for you, then try writing it down: all the pity, the sorrow, the rage, the feelings. Writing will release it for you. Write, talk, exercise, bang a pillow, or confide in a trusted source. Do not include those who have hurt you; do not reach out to them, not at this point. By engaging with those who hurt you at this point, it can do you more damage than you deserve. Do not take it out on innocent others; this is your healing and you do not need to offload your anguish onto another. There are ways to release and not hurt anyone, including yourself, in the process.

THE "WHY" QUESTION PROCESS

I was writing quite a bit during my healing and one process that was a huge help for me was the "Why" Question Process. It helped me uncover deep layers within. Layers that hid under the shallow surfaces. There was more to the story than I realized. The best way to understand the process is to see it in action. It is best to start with questions using the word "Why". Do not hesitate to answer. The trick is to write or type what first comes into your mind. Do not discredit or doubt your responses. This exercise needs to flow without interruption from your brain. Let the answers flow easily and without hesitation or question.

For example, let's say someone has a confidence problem. They lack self-confidence, self-worth, and low self-esteem. For this example, let's concentrate on lack of self-confidence. How do we rid ourselves of this belief? Where did it come from? You have a belief within that you are an underqualified person. This belief is way down deep inside and has fastened itself to you. Are you doomed with this forever? No. Is there a way to get rid of this parasite? Yes, but only if you truly and sincerely want to. Without desire, drive and determination, you will not get very far.

You need to do the "Why?" process. You ask yourself a question, then you answer it. Then you ask a question about the answer. Then you answer that question. Then you ask a question about that answer.... You will be amazed at what you discover within yourself. Take your time. Keep going deeper and deeper until you get to the core, to the source of your belief. Trust that you will know when you see it. It can be like a light bulb going off inside your brain. Once you have the source of your belief, you can then start the undoing, unlearning, and creating process.

With pen and paper, or keyboard, write down "Why do I lack self-confidence?" The following is an example of the "Why" process and may not be your answers. I am giving a fictional sample of how it works.

> *Why do I lack self-confidence?*
> I don't know, I just do,
>
> *Do you remember the first time you experienced it?*
> As a kid when I took dance lessons.
>
> *What happened?*
> This other girl was so good, and I was lousy.
>
> *Why do I think I was lousy? Did someone tell me I was lousy?*
> No, no one told me. I thought I was lousy because she was better.
>
> *Okay, she was better, but is it fair to say I was lousy?*
> No, it isn't.
>
> *If you were an adult watching a bunch of 2 and 3 year olds dance, would you think any of them were lousy?*
> No of course not, they are just learning how to dance.

So perhaps I placed high expectations on myself even at that age?
Yes, I think I did.

Why such a need for high expectations at such a young age?
I wanted to be perfect, the best, to please my mom, to be like my mom.

Why such a need to be perfect, or to please mom or whatever?
Because my dad always told me to "make mama proud".

Why make Mama proud?
That was my father's thing, always telling me that.

Perhaps I took it too seriously since he said it all the time?
Perhaps

Perhaps it caused me to place a too high demand on myself?
Perhaps

Did you think my mother would love me less if I failed?
Not at all, I just wanted my mother to be proud of me.

Do I think she is proud of me now and always?
Yes, she was always proud of me except the times I screwed up.

How did I feel when I upset her?
I felt very, very low. I hated upsetting her; it bothered me horribly.

We all make mistakes including my mother; can I accept that?
Yes

Can my mother accept it?
Of course, she didn't love me any less, she didn't attack me; she attacked my behavior.

So now that I know my father instilled this belief in me to "Always make mama proud", do I still need to believe this and act on it in overcompensating ways?
I want my mom to be proud of me, which is important to me, but if I screw up that is part of being human, we all make mistakes. Always is a heavy word to press upon a kid, I can see that now.

Am I willing to be okay when I make mistakes and know that my mom will still love me regardless?
Yes

Am I willing to release this belief that I "must always make my mother proud"?
Yes I am; it is a huge burden lifted. I am willing to believe my mom is always proud of me. I know she loves me and part of loving me includes being proud of me. I accept that now.

If asking more questions and "Why" questions are needed than keep asking. Keep asking until you cannot answer, not because the answer may hurt, but because you cannot answer anymore. You are at the core, the source. You will know with an instinctive knowing. You know when you hit the core.

Referring to the sample above, was this father being malicious when he said that again and again to his daughter? Absolutely not. Was he using the word "always" to purposely scare her into behaving properly? Probably not. Maybe he was trying to teach his daughter to be a good person. Did his daughter take his words seriously and to heart? That's what children do. This expression was repeated frequently over the years to the daughter until it was ingrained in her brain – it wasn't said once or twice. Children are vulnerable though, saying or doing something even a few times can have a life-long impact.

We do not always get false beliefs from malicious, evil people who intend to do us harm. Sometimes it is the simplest of expressions, with the most innocent of intentions that can be misunderstood by a child. No one's fault, no one is wrong – it just needs fixing. So for those of you that did not have caretakers who abused you, it could be the repeated innocent comments, beliefs and scare tactics to make you obey that got you off course. So does this mean we stop telling our children anything for fear of causing an overreaction in them later on in life? Not at all. But perhaps as parents and guardians we could choose our words with care and words that are age appropriate. Will we still screw it up? Probably. But much can be overcome when the child feels unconditional love. And love, along with education, goes a lot further than lashing out with false beliefs to get a child to obey.

THERAPY/SUPPORT SYSTEMS

Various forms of therapy and support systems have helped vast amounts of people over the years. They also haven't helped. Friends and family can be a great source of support but they cannot always provide an unbiased viewpoint. Nor are they qualified. Certain support groups rehash over and over what happened and keep you in victim status. People have healed exclusively on their own. Quality therapy and/or support systems are invaluable tools that help you on your journey. What is crucial though, is the quality of the therapy and support system.

Before you join a group or go to a therapist, you need to ask yourself what it is you are looking for. Do you want others to listen? Do you need guidance? Does being with others make you feel less alone during your healing? Are the feelings so overwhelming that you need professional assistance to guide you? Do you have a certain condition you want to address?

Even if you are not sure what you need, do not let that stop you from reaching out. It is important to know their background, experience and goals. What is the mission statement of the group? What is the goal of the group? Does it seek to improve its members by education and/or sharing experiences? Does it aim to enlighten, enhance, and improve your state of being?

Does it drone with a never-ending saga of "poor me"? Is the foundation of the group to just keep rehashing events over and over?

Talk with the organizer of the group; ask questions pertinent to you and what you are looking for. Do not be afraid to interview prospective organizations that you think can help you. You want to be in a group that progresses and not one that stays stagnant. Get in groups that address you as a person - your behavior, your reactions, what can you change about you?

Various factors are included with seeing a therapist. Is the person in your insurance plan and if not, what kind of payment plans/options do they offer? Do you want a specific gender and/or a certain age range? You want someone who has experience with your needs. For example, if you suffer from panic or anxiety, find a therapist who has expertise in this area. Ask them what their specialty is and how much experience they have treating clients with anxiety disorders. The internet, library, hospitals, and some towns are all great resources for acquiring lists of groups and/or therapists applicable to your needs. If using someone via the computer and perhaps in another state, ask to see their credentials, by law it must be displayed.

When I was looking for a therapist I called a group of women in an upscale neighborhood thinking they must be good since they are located in an expensive town. Before I could get a word out, the woman on the other end of the phone told me that whatever drug I wanted I could have. I wasn't interested in drugs, I wanted to get better, but she seemed disinterested in helping me heal. She seemed more interested in letting me know any drug I wanted was available. Needless to say, I crossed that practice off my list.

If you do go, and are not comfortable with the group or therapist the first time try to determine the source of your unease. Is it because you feel there was no connection, a lack of knowledge on the part of the group or therapist, or is fear causing resistance? If you can, try to go a few times before you make your final decision. I went to a therapist for anxiety and when I left I was undecided if I was going to go back. I didn't feel comfortable. I was resisting the entire process. I gave him another chance though and I continued with him. He did help me and I have recommended him to others. It was my resistance that made me uncomfortable.

So maybe you could try it a few times and then decide whether to continue or not. If someone came to your home and did a lousy job would you hire him or her again? Of course not. The same decision should be applied with your group or therapist. If it isn't working to your liking, find another. Talk with trusted others as you go through the process; find like-minded people to share your thoughts with. You do not have to go it alone; know there are many avenues to choose from. Just make sure these others help you to succeed, and not drag you down.

Writing Your Feelings/ Journaling

I have found that people either hate writing or they love it. I have also found that those who hate it, but tried it, felt better afterwards. It helps to release pent-up energy, emotions, and feelings. There are numerous outlets for pent-up emotion: writing, talking, exercising, punching a pillow, doing something creative, etc. Writing/typing provides a release and that is our goal – to release all the stored memories and emotions haunting us today.

It is important to write down what you are feeling and not just what the person who hurt you did or didn't do. Writing about the experience helps, but the real release comes when you write your feelings. Writing a letter to the person who hurt you helps, but do not mail the letter or send it to them. The letter is strictly to allow the feelings to come up and out. Get as explicit as need be and without guilt. No one will see the letter or your writings. Perhaps you are writing about guilt or regret over something you did to someone and are working on forgiving yourself. Putting it down on paper and being able to read it will do wonders for your healing. Remember to write the feelings you feel and not what happened.

"I feel sad, rejected, abandoned, angry, enraged, hurt, ripped-off, taken advantage of, etc." I was so enraged one time all I wrote was "I _____ hate you!" over and over, page after page.

Don't hold back, get it all out, and let that pen fly across that paper or let your keystrokes go crazy with feeling. Release it, get it out, it is only doing damage by remaining inside you. It is not worth getting sick over, you deserve so much more. Do not forget current feelings; do not let them fester and contaminate within like your childhood feelings.

I used writing to bring up past memories that needed to surface so I could heal from them. I would either write or type depending on my mood and just let whatever that needed to come up and out do so. As I relaxed into it and allowed the words to flow onto the paper, thoughts, memories, and details just seemed to come out of nowhere. Writing was an invaluable tool for me when I needed to nudge up feelings and memories that were stuck. The writing allowed the repressions in my body to loosen and surface.

You are doing these exercises to release feelings and emotions that are repressed. This is not about blaming or self-pity. There is no need to feel guilty because you feel anger towards a parent. The goal is to release the anger and pain. When you are no longer glued and stuck on these feelings, your understanding of that parent, spouse, caretaker, whoever, will increase. Your compassion will rise since you see the position they were in. You may or may not like them, that's fine, but your understanding of what happened to you will be clearer. After you process all the hurts and pain, all the hate and rage, then forgiveness will seep into those hollowed out places within where those repressed feelings use to be. And that is permanent change.

AFTERWORD

I hope you find *Series 1 - The Groundwork Guidebook* an invaluable reference tool on your journey. *Series 2 – The Foundation Guidebook* begins detailed descriptions of what I have learned during my transformation. *The Foundation Guidebook* will cover "Beating Yourself Up", "Body Talk", "Emotions" and other topics in greater detail. The need to stop beating yourself up is crucial on your healing path and needs to be cleared away.

We are just beginning the process of digging ourselves out. I use myself and my journey as the example. We are at different levels of experience of being wronged, from unintentional mistreatment to full blown abuse. Within these pages, I pray that everyone of all ages and at whatever level, will find for themselves, a discovery that sets them free.

Let your story begin....

About the Author

Virginia Anne has made great strides in overcoming early childhood abuse. She discovered a process that allowed her to heal and uses this process with others successfully. With the help of a licensed professional, she transformed her life. Virginia Anne enjoys creating affirmations for herself and others and is from New Jersey.

Printed in the United States
By Bookmasters